Power-Up College English

<Intro>

パワーアップ・イングリッシュ
〈入門編〉

JACET リスニング研究会

南雲堂

NAN'UN-DO

Power-Up College English <Intro>

パワーアップ・イングリッシュ〈入門編〉

by

JACET SIG on Listening

Download Audio

音声ファイル
無料 DL
のご案内

このテキストの音声を無料で視聴（ストリーミング）・ダウンロードできます。自習用音声としてご活用ください。
以下のサイトにアクセスしてテキスト番号で検索してください。

https://nanun-do.com テキスト番号［**498056**］

※ 無線 LAN（WiFi）に接続してのご利用を推奨いたします。

※ 音声ダウンロードは Zip ファイルでの提供になります。
お使いの機器によっては別途ソフトウェア（アプリケーション）の導入が必要となります。

Read by
Karen Haedrich（アメリカ英語）
Josh Keller（アメリカ英語）

※ Power-Up College English <Intro> の音声ダウンロードページは以下の QR コードからもご利用になれます。

はじめに

本書『パワーアップ･イングリッシュ ＜入門編＞』は、ロングセラーを続けているパワーアップシリーズの姉妹編となる **Nan'un-do Semester Series** ***Power-Up College English*** 第 2 作目にあたります。大学生としてぜひ身につけておきたい英語力（聴解力、読解力、会話力、文法力、および作文力）の基礎を積極的に学習できるよう配慮された、まさにオールラウンドな英語教材です。本書は中・高の復習を主眼としていますが、Reading Passage だけは大学生の知的レベルに配慮した構成になっています。

本書の特徴は次の 3 つです。

(1) トピックは、身近な話題「趣味」「スポーツ」「旅行」から、大学生として理解を深めておきたい話題「教育」「言語」「社会・環境問題」に至るまで多岐にわたり、リスニング、リーディング、及びライティングの 3 つのセクションではユニットごとにトピックに関連性を持たせています。従って、学習者は学びやすく、興味・関心を持って問題に取り組むことができます。

(2) Writing Section では、Exercise 1、2 においては、部分英作文を取り入れています。また、Exercise 3 においては、同じ Unit の Reading Passage の一部（太字部分）を参考にして和文英訳をしていきます。英語のアウトプットは例文・連語・構文等のインプット（暗記）に始まるからです。実際の作業は、主として数語を入れ替えるという単純なものですが、結果だけを見れば、10 語を超える英文を記述することになり、「英語を書いた」という達成感が得られます。

(3) Speaking Section では、日常生活における様々な場面において想定される、“決まり文句”を伴う対話をとりあげました。無造作に棒読みをしたり、一途に暗記するのではなく、語句の発音や強勢の位置を意識して、正しいイントネーションを伴った発話を求めています。また、日本語を見て、それを英語に置き換えることで、自然と英文が頭の中に構築され、その英文が抵抗なく自分の言葉として発話されることをねらいとしています。学習の際、日本語を見ながら何度も英語音声を聞き、発話した後で、学習者自らがサイトトランスレーション（後ろから前に戻らずに、文を文頭から区切って訳す方法）を行えば、自然なスピーキングへの橋渡しになります。

刊行にあたり、南雲堂編集部の加藤 敦氏、英文校閲などを担当していただきました Jim Knudsen 氏に大変お世話になりました。ここに深く感謝の意を表します。

2020年 8月

執筆者一同

本書の構成と学び方

本書は全 14 ユニット（各ユニット 4 ページ仕立て）の構成で、半期用に対応できるように編集されています。各ユニットは 5 セクションから成り立ち、各ユニットのフォーマットを統一したことで、学習計画が立てやすく、授業展開もスムーズに進められます。

◉ Listening Section

◆ *Listening Points*

リスニング力の向上に役立つコツやヒントを用例付きで紹介しています。

◆ Exercise 1

「絵」について、3 つの短い描写文を聞き、正しく叙述している文を選びます。

◆ Exercise 2

発話とそれに対する 3 つの応答を聞き、発話に最もふさわしい応答を 1 つ選びます。

◆ Exercise 3

50 語程度の英文を聞き、その内容について記載された 2 つの設問に答えます。

◉ Reading Section

◆ *Words & Phrases*

Reading Passage より抜粋された語（句）に一致する日本語訳を選択します。

◆ *Reading Passage*

各ユニットのトピックに関連した題材を取り上げて、180 語程度で書かれた英文です。

◆ Exercise 1

空所補充の問題形式で本文の内容理解を深めます。

◆ Exercise 2

本文の内容について記述された英文の真偽を問う問題で、内容の理解度を確かめます。

◉ Grammar Section

◆ **Exercise 1**

標記の文法項目について、空所に入る適切な語句を選択肢の中から選びます。

◆ **Exercise 2**

標記の文法項目に基づいた空所補充問題で、文法力の基礎を習得するのに効果的です。

◉ Writing Section

◆ **Exercise 1**

空所に適語を補って英文を完成させます。

◆ **Exercise 2**

与えられた日本文に合うように、与えられた語を正しく並べ替えて英文を完成させます。

◆ **Exercise 3**

Reading Passage の一部（太字部分）を参考に、和文英訳により作文力の向上を図ります。

◉ Speaking Section

◆ **Exercise 1**

英語の強く発音するところを黒く塗り、英語の正しいリズム感を理論立てて学びます。

◆ **Exercise 2**

日本語を見て、英語を聞き話すことでスピーキング力 の基礎を養います。

◆ **Exercise 3**

短い対話形式で発話を楽しみながら、日常生活における感情表現を自然と身につけます。

◉ Appendix

文法項目が要領よくまとめてあります。予習や復習など、自主学習にも役立ちます。

CONTENTS

Unit 1 Self-Introduction

● Listening Section ● 2

Listening Points

英語のリズム（1）—強く発音されるのはどこ？—

英語のリズムは、音の強勢が周期的に繰り返されることにより構成されています。一般的に、内容語（名詞、一般動詞、形容詞、副詞、数詞、疑問詞など）は強く発音され（●表示）、機能語（be 動詞、助動詞、冠詞、人称代名詞、前置詞、接続詞など）は弱く発音されます（○表示）。

1. study
●

2. sorry
●

3. in the morning
○ ○ ●

4. at the cafeteria
○ ○ ●

5. I'm a student at Reiwa University.
○ ○ ● ○ ● ●

Exercise 1 CD を聞いて、絵について正しく描写している英文を選びなさい。 3

1. (a) (b) (c)

2. (a) (b) (c)

Exercise 2 CD を聞いて、質問に対する最も適切な応答を選びなさい。 4

1. (a) Thanks. (b) I'm fine. (c) Nice to meet you, too.
2. (a) All right. (b) Go ahead. (c) Yes, you can.

Exercise 3 CD を聞いて、次の設問に答えなさい。 5

1. Where is the woman going?
   (a) Reiwa Senior High School.
   (b) Reiwa University.
   (c) California.
2. Where is the man from?
   (a) He is from Canada.
   (b) He is from the United States.
   (c) He is from Japan.

● Reading Section ●

Hiro's Self-Introduction

Words & Phrases 次の語句の日本語訳を選びなさい。

1. introduce ( ) 2. freshman ( ) 3. major ( ) 4. travel ( )
5. foreign ( ) 6. in particular ( ) 7. learn ( ) 8. future ( )
9. tourism ( ) 10. familiar with ( )

(a) 専攻する (b) 外国の (c) 特に (d) 学ぶ (e) よく知っている
(f) 観光業 (g) 新入生 (h) 将来 (i) 旅行する (j) 紹介する

6

Reading Passage

Hello, everyone. Let me introduce myself. My name is Yoshino Hiroshi. Please call me Hiro. I'm a freshman at this university and major in business administration. I have signed up for the swimming club. I was born in Tokyo but live in Kobe now.

I love to travel and have been to many famous sightseeing spots around Japan. But I have never been to a foreign country, so I really want to go someday. In particular, I'd like to visit Australia, because it has so many beautiful beaches.

I hope to learn a lot about business administration at this university and, after graduation, work in the travel industry. In the future, I'd like to start a tourism business of my own.

Lastly, I'd like to make as many friends as possible. **My home is near this university, so I'm familiar with this area.** If you want to know the best places to eat or shop, I would be happy to show you around. Thank you.

(166 words)

business administration 経営学　sign up for（クラブなどに）加入する　sightseeing（場所の）観光
have been to ~ ～へ行ったことがある　I'd like to ~ 私は～したいと思う　after graduation 卒業後
of one's own 自分自身の　lastly 最後に　make as many friends as possible できるだけ多くの友達を作る
show around 案内する

Exercise 1 （　）内に最も適切な語句を選んで、文を完成させなさい。

1. Hiro is a(n) (　　　　　　　　) of the swimming club.
   (a) member　(b) owner　(c) trainer
2. Hiro is originally from (　　　　　　　　).
   (a) Australia　(b) Kobe　(c) Tokyo
3. Hiro enjoys (　　　　　　　　).
   (a) drawing and painting　(b) taking trips　(c) shopping on the Internet

Exercise 2 次の各文が本文の内容に合っていれば T(True)、合っていなければ F(False) と書きなさい。

____ 1. Hiro wants to visit Australia because he has many friends there.
____ 2. Hiro is planning to study business administration at the university.
____ 3. Hiro's dream for the future is to have his own company.

● Grammar Section ●

名詞・代名詞

Grammar Points

1. 名詞には数えられる名詞と数えられない名詞があり、文中で主語、目的語、補語になります。
   That is a **dog**.　数えられて単数形と複数形があり、*a dog*（犬）は単数扱いです（普通名詞）。
   There is no **water** to drink.　「水」はそのままでは数えられず、単数扱いです（物質名詞）。
   The **police** are after you.　集合体をさし、*the police*（警察）は複数扱いです（集合名詞）。
2. 人称代名詞には、一人称、二人称、三人称と単数、複数の区別があり、格変化（主格、所有格、目的格）をします（I, my, me など）。また、所有代名詞、再帰代名詞の形もあります。
   This is my book and that is **yours**.　所有代名詞で、「～のもの」という意味になります。
   Jim blamed **himself.**　再帰代名詞で、「～自身（自分）」という意味になります。

Exercise 1 （　）内に入る最も適切な語（句）を選びなさい。

1. I always wear (glass / a glass / glasses).
2. I stopped drinking alcohol on my doctor's (advice / advices / advise).
3. I have an (interest / interesting / interested) in photography.

Exercise 2 下線部の語句の代わりとなるように、次の（　）内に適切な代名詞を入れなさい。

1. This is <u>Ms. Li</u>. (　　　　　　　　) is a friend of mine from China.
2. I have <u>some beautiful pet fish</u>. I like (　　　　　　　　) very much.
3. <u>My children</u> can speak English fluently. I'm so proud of (　　　　　　　　).

● Writing Section ●

「自己紹介」に関わる表現

Exercise 1 下の語群から適当な名詞を選んで、文を完成させなさい。

1. There are four members in my (　　　　　　　　　　).
2. My (　　　　　　　　　　) both work.
3. I major in (　　　　　　　　　　).

family	mathematics	parents

Exercise 2 (　) 内の語を並べかえて英文を完成させなさい。

1. うちは大家族です。(family / is / my)

   ________________________________ a large one.

2. 私はたいてい朝食にトーストを１枚食べます。(toast / slice / of)

   I usually have a ________________________________ for breakfast.

3. 母は 20 代の頃、有名な美女でした。(famous / a / beauty)

   My mother was ________________________________ in her 20s.

Exercise 3 日本文を英語に直しなさい。

私はこの公園の近くに住んでいますので、この地域のことはよく知っています。

____

● Speaking Section ●

「自己紹介」の表現

7

Exercise 1 強く発音するところの○を黒く塗りつぶしなさい。次に CD を聞いてリピートし、英文を覚えなさい。

1. A: Hello. **Let me introduce myself. I'm** Ken. **I'm from** Kobe.

   ○ ○ ○ ○ ○ ○ ○ ○ ○ ○

   B: Hi, Ken. **I'm** Nancy. I'm glad to meet you.

   ○ ○ ○ ○ ○ ○ ○ ○ ○

2. A: Hello. **My name is** Kato Taro. **I'm a** freshman at Reiwa University.

   ○ ○ ○ ○ ○ ○ ○ ○ ○ ○ ○ ○

   B: Hi, **I'm** Mary Smith. Nice to meet you.

   ○○ ○ ○ ○ ○ ○ ○

Exercise 2 日本語を参考にして、英語で言ってみましょう。

1. A: こんにちは。自己紹介させていただきます。ケンと申します。神戸出身です。

   B: はじめまして、ケンさん。ナンシーです。お会いできてうれしいです。

2. A: こんにちは。カトウ・タロウと申します。令和大学の１年生です。

   B: はじめまして、メアリー・スミスです。よろしくお願いします。

Exercise 3 Exercise 1 の会話をペアで練習しなさい。

Unit 2 Hobbies

● Listening Section ●

8

Listening Points

英語のリズム（2）―強く発音される who はどっち？―

下の文 1 では、who に強勢が置かれますが、2 では who に強勢は置かれません。これは 1 の who は疑問詞（内容語）であり、2 の who は関係代名詞 (機能語) であるためです。

1. Who made the cake?
   ● ● ○ ●

2. I know the student who made the cake.
   ○ ● ○ ● ○ ● ○ ●

Exercise 1 CD を聞いて、絵について正しく描写している英文を選びなさい。 9

1. (a) (b) (c)　　　2. (a) (b) (c)

Exercise 2 CD を聞いて、質問に対する最も適切な応答を選びなさい。 10

1. (a) I'm free this afternoon.　(b) I like to read detective novels.　(c) No, I don't.
2. (a) I play the piano.　(b) I don't think so.　(c) I like jazz.

Exercise 3 CD を聞いて、次の設問に答えなさい。 11

1. What are they going to do this weekend?
   (a) They are going hiking.
   (b) They are going to work on a class project.
   (c) They are going to do their homework.

2. What season is it?
   (a) It's spring.
   (b) It's summer.
   (c) It's fall.

● Reading Section ●

A Speech about Hobbies

Words & Phrases 次の語句の日本語訳を選びなさい。

1. pastime ( ) 2. impressive ( ) 3. experience ( ) 4. countryside ( )
5. realistic ( ) 6. movement ( ) 7. smell ( ) 8. vocabulary ( )
9. expression ( ) 10. subtitle ( )

(a) 語彙 (b) 経験する (c) (言葉の) 言い回し (d) 娯楽 (e) 字幕
(f) 現実的な (g) 田舎 (h) においを嗅ぐ (i) 印象的な (j) 動き

12

Reading Passage

What is your hobby or pastime? As for me, **I enjoy watching movies in my free time,** and that's what I would like to talk to you about today—movies.

I especially enjoy watching action movies in the theater. Action films are so impressive. You can virtually experience soaring across the sky or driving through a city or the countryside at a high speed. 4D movies are especially great. They help make your moviegoing experience more realistic and exciting. Sometimes, you can even feel some movement or smell something that is being shown on the screen.

I also watch a lot of movies online or on DVD. Movies are a great way to learn English and about other cultures. When I like a movie, I try to watch it over and over several times to learn vocabulary, useful idiomatic expressions, gestures and body language.

Those are just some reasons why I like movies. I plan to watch more of them and learn a lot as I do. My goal is to be able to watch English movies without subtitles. Thank you for listening.

(183 words)

especially 特に　virtually あたかも実体験しているように　soar 空高く飛ぶ　4D (four-dimensional) 4次元の
moviegoing 映画館通いをする　idiomatic 慣用的な　gesture ジェスチャー　body language 身ぶり言語

Exercise 1 (　) 内に最も適切な語を選んで、文を完成させなさい。

1. The person's speech is mainly about (　　　　　　　　).
   (a) culture　　(b) movies　　(c) English
2. In 4D movies, you might feel or (　　　　　　　　) something.
   (a) smell　　(b) touch　　(c) taste
3. The speaker watches movies in theaters as well as on DVD and (　　　　　　　　).
   (a) TV　　(b) blu-ray　　(c) online

Exercise 2 次の各文が本文の内容に合っていれば T(True)、合っていなければ F(False) と書きなさい。

____ 1. The speaker thinks watching romantic movies in theaters is very impressive.
____ 2. Not only can you learn English from watching movies, but you can also learn about other cultures.
____ 3. The speaker can understand movies in English without reading subtitles.

● Grammar Section ●

5 文型

Grammar Points

英文には 5 つの文型があります。(S 主語、V 動詞、C 補語、O 目的語)

第 1 文型	(SV)	I go to movies.	(S = I, V = go)
第 2 文型	(SVC)	Movies are fun.	(S= Movies, V = are, C = fun)
第 3 文型	(SVO)	I like movies.	(S = I, V = like, O = movies)
第 4 文型	(SVOO)	I bought him a DVD.	(S = I, V = bought, O = him, O = a DVD)
第 5 文型	(SVOC)	The movie made me laugh.	(S = The movie, V = made, O = me, C = laugh)

Exercise 1 (　) 内に入る最も適切な語を選びなさい。

1. I (enjoy / give / let) traveling.
2. Playing video games for a long time (is / lets / keeps) bad for your eyes.
3. I (thought / found / had) this book interesting.

Exercise 2 次の文の文型を答えなさい。

1. My brother gave me this CD.　　第 (　　) 文型
2. I often go to the movies.　　第 (　　) 文型
3. Working out made me tired.　　第 (　　) 文型

● Writing Section ●

「趣味」に関わる表現

Exercise 1 下の語群から適当な語を選んで、文を完成させなさい。

1. My hobby (　　　　　　　　) playing tennis.
2. He (　　　　　　　　) playing the guitar.
3. She is (　　　　　　　　) in going to museums.

interested	is	likes

Exercise 2 (　) 内の語を並べかえて英文を完成させなさい。

1. あなたの趣味は何ですか。(hobby / your / is)
   What ________________________________?
2. 私は、長期休暇の時に旅行するのが好きです。(traveling / like / during)
   I ________________________________ my long vacations.
3. 散歩は楽しいし、健康に良い。(fun / good / and)
   Walking is ________________________________ for your health.

Exercise 3 日本文を英語に直しなさい。

私は暇な時に、読書を楽しみます。

____

● Speaking Section ●

「出会い」の表現

13

Exercise 1 強く発音するところの○を黒く塗りつぶしなさい。次に CD を聞いてリピートし、英文を覚えなさい。

1. A: Hi, Andy. **Long time no see.**
   ○○ ○ ○ ○ ○
   B: Yeah, I know. You look great.
   ○ ○ ○ ○ ○ ○
2. A: Good morning, Emma. **What's new?**
   ○ ○ ○ ○ ○
   B: Not much. Just doing the same old thing.
   ○ ○ ○ ○ ○○ ○ ○

Exercise 2 日本語を参考にして、英語で言ってみましょう。

1. A: やあ、アンディ。お久しぶり。
   B: そうだね。元気そうだね。
2. A: おはよう、エマ。最近どう?
   B: 特に何も。いつもと変わりないよ。

Exercise 3 Exercise 1 の会話をペアで練習しなさい。

Unit 3 Food and Exercise

● Listening Section ●

14

Listening Points

意味のグループ単位での理解 ―音声を聞く時の区切りはどこ？―

英文は小さな意味のまとまり（センスグループ）に分けることができます。そのまとまりごとに区切り、文頭から「英語の語順」のまま意味を取って聞きましょう。

Next time /	I see you /	in the gym, /	I'll show you /	how to use machines.
次回 /	あなたにお会いしたら /	ジムで /	教えてあげます /	機械の使い方を。

Exercise 1 CD を聞いて、絵について正しく描写している英文を選びなさい。 15

1. (a) (b) (c)

2. (a) (b) (c)

Exercise 2 CD を聞いて、質問に対する最も適切な応答を選びなさい。 16

1. (a) I'm fine. (b) Me, too. (c) Yes, thank you.

2. (a) So do I. (b) Yes, I do. (c) Sounds good.

Exercise 3 CD を聞いて、次の設問に答えなさい。 17

1. What does the woman know how to do?
   (a) Make Italian dishes.
   (b) Make a popular Japanese food.
   (c) Make popular sweets.

2. When will the woman bring the recipe?
   (a) The next day.
   (b) Next Monday.
   (c) Next Friday.

● Reading Section ●

Food and Exercise

Words & Phrases 次の語句の日本語訳を選びなさい。

1. run into (　)　2. expect (　)　3. keep fit (　)　4. diet (　)
5. mean (　)　6. lose weight (　)　7. contain (　)　8. protein (　)
9. low-fat (　)　10. nutritional (　)

(a) 栄養の　(b) 意味する　(c) 体重を落とす　(d) ばったり会う　(e) 低脂肪の
(f) 食事、食生活　(g) 健康を保つ　(h) タンパク質　(i) 予期する　(j) 含む

18

Reading Passage

Jane is jogging along Pine Street. She runs into a friend of hers.

Jane ： Good morning, Hiro.

Hiro ： Oh, hi, Jane. Fancy meeting you here! I never expected to see you so early in the morning. Do you run every day?

Jane ： Yes. I run here every morning, unless it rains. You know, for my health.

Hiro ： Well, it's working. You look great! Are you doing anything else to keep fit?

Jane ： Yes. I'm trying to keep a healthy diet.

Hiro ： Diet? What do you mean? Do you want to lose weight?

Jane ： No, that's not what I mean. The word "diet" also means the kinds of food we eat.

Hiro ： Now I understand. What kinds of food do you eat then?

Jane ： Lots of fresh vegetables and foods that contain a lot of protein such as *tofu* and low-fat meat. **I'm really careful about nutritional balance.**

Hiro ： Good for you! I have to take better care of my health, too.

(161 words)

Fancy meeting you here　奇遇ですね　　unless ~ ～でない限り　　you know（話題の対象を明確にするために）「ほら」「あれだよ」　　work（計画などが）うまくいく　　Good for you（人の行動などに納得して）よかった、偉い　　take better care of my health　もっと自分の健康に気をつける

Exercise 1 (　) 内に最も適切な語句を選んで、文を完成させなさい。

1. Jane is running on Pine Street (　　　　　　　　　　).
   (a) with Hiro　(b) with a classmate　(c) by herself
2. A good diet means (　　　　　　　　　　).
   (a) eating healthy foods　(b) losing weight　(c) getting lots of exercise
3. *Tofu* is rich in (　　　　　　　　).
   (a) protein　(b) flavor　(c) fat

Exercise 2 次の各文が本文の内容に合っていれば T(True)、合っていなければ F(False) と書きなさい。

____ 1. Jane runs on Pine Street even if it rains.

____ 2. Jane is on a diet because she is trying to lose weight.

____ 3. Jane eats low-fat meat because it is good for her health.

● Grammar Section ●

現在・過去・未来

Grammar Points

英語には現在時制と過去時制の２種類に加えて、未来を表す表現形式があります。

① Our school **stands** on a hill.（現在の状態）

② I always **drink** a cup of coffee in the morning.（現在の習慣）

③ Please call me as soon as Jim **comes**.（現在時制で未来の事柄）

④ Lisa **liked** playing the piano.（過去の状態）

⑤ I **ran** for an hour.（過去の動作）

⑥ I **will go** to New York to meet a friend of mine.（意思）

⑦ I **am going to join** a professional volleyball team after graduation from college.（未来の予定）

Exercise 1 (　) 内に入る最も適切な語 (句) を選びなさい。

1. She (eats / is eating) breakfast every morning.
2. When we (came / come) home, dinner was already made.
3. I (starting / will start) taking dancing lessons next year.

Exercise 2 (　) 内の語を必要に応じて適切な形に直しなさい。

1. I (do) my best in the 100-meter dash tomorrow. ____________
2. When you (arrive) at the restaurant, please let me know. ____________
3. She (bake) some chocolate chip cookies for her daughter yesterday. ____________

● Writing Section ●

「食べ物・運動」に関わる表現

Exercise 1 下の語群から適当な語（句）を選んで、文を完成しなさい。

1. Walking every morning (   ) feel better.
2. Oranges (   ) lots of vitamin C.
3. I (   ) an aerobics class yesterday.

contain	took	will make you

Exercise 2 （ ）内の語を並べかえて英文を完成させなさい。

1. 筋肉をつけることが必要です。(up / to / build)
   It is necessary________________________ your muscles.
2. その店はおいしいチーズケーキで有名でした。(for / was / famous)
   That store ________________________ its delicious cheesecake.
3. 自然食品がその新しくできた店で売られるでしょう。(sold / be / will)
   Organic foods ________________________ in the new store.

Exercise 3 日本文を英語に直しなさい。

私たちが食べる食べ物の栄養についても、気を付けなければならない。(栄養　nutritional value)

____

● Speaking Section ●

「見舞い」の表現

19

Exercise 1 強く発音するところの○を黒く塗りつぶしなさい。次に CD を聞いてリピートし、英文を覚えなさい。

1. A: Did you know that John is in the hospital? I'm worried about him.
   ○ ○ ○ ○ ○ ○○ ○ ○ ○ ○ ○ ○
   B: Really? I didn't know that. **We should call on him.**
   ○ ○○ ○ ○ ○ ○ ○○ ○
2. A: I've had a bad cold since last Thursday. I have a fever.
   ○ ○ ○ ○ ○ ○ ○ ○ ○○ ○○
   B: **That's too bad. I hope you'll get better soon.**
   ○ ○ ○ ○ ○ ○ ○ ○ ○

Exercise 2 日本語を参考にして、英語で言ってみましょう。

1. A: ジョンが入院していることを知っていましたか。彼のことが心配です。
   B: 本当ですか。知らなかったです。お見舞いに行かなければならないですね。
2. A: 先週の木曜日からひどい風邪を引いています。熱があります。
   B: それはいけないですね。早く、よくなるといいですね。

Exercise 3 Exercise 1 の会話をペアで練習しなさい。

Unit 4 Sports (Rugby)

● Listening Section ●

20

Listening Points

消える音に慣れる (1) —Very sad. はどう聞こえる？—

[d] [t] [b] [p] [g] [k] などは、語末、句末、文末では聞こえにくくなることがあります。

1. bed / hat / Bob / stop / bag / kick
2. at last / from behind / for a week
3. What a cute dog! / That's too bad! / Watch your step!

Exercise 1 CD を聞いて、絵について正しく描写している英文を選びなさい。 21

1. (a) (b) (c)

2. (a) (b) (c)

Exercise 2 CD を聞いて、質問に対する最も適切な応答を選びなさい。 22

1. (a) I like tennis. (b) I'll think about it. (c) I'm a member of the swimming club.
2. (a) Sure. (b) Go ahead. (c) Yes, you could.

Exercise 3 CD を聞いて、次の設問に答えなさい。 23

1. What sport does the man like?
   (a) Baseball.
   (b) Rugby and baseball.
   (c) He prefers night games.

2. How did the baseball game come out?
   (a) The other team won by a score of three to one.
   (b) His favorite team lost by a score of one to three.
   (c) His favorite team won by a score of three to one.

● Reading Section ●

"One Team"

Words & Phrases 次の語句の日本語訳を選びなさい。

1. represent (　)　2. take part (　)　3. cheer (　)　4. powerful (　)
5. delighted (　)　6. spread (　)　7. propose (　)　8. encourage (　)
9. ordinarily (　)　10. overcome (　)

(a) 声援を送る　(b) 克服する　(c) 強力な　(d) 広がる　(e) 勇気づける
(f) 提案する　(g) 喜んで　(h) 参加する　(i) 通常　(j) 代表する

24

Reading Passage

Rugby World Cup 2019 was held in Japan for the first time in the autumn of 2019. Twenty teams representing each region of the world took part. We all watched the games in stadiums and on TV, cheering on the Japanese team. Our team played very well against the world's most powerful teams and made it to the Best 8. We were delighted, and "rugby fever" spread around the country very quickly. The Japanese team's slogan was "One Team." It had been proposed as a catchphrase by the team's head coach to encourage his players, and was later selected as the Word of the Year for the New and Buzz Word Grand Prix.

Ordinarily, "one team" is synonymous with "a team." But to the Japanese team in 2019, the phrase had a special, much deeper meaning. Nearly half of the team's 31 players were from foreign countries. When we knew this, the slogan used by the Japanese team shone so brightly. It meant that Japan would play all its games as a team that would overcome differences of place of birth, culture, beliefs, and lifestyle to become one."

(219 words)

make it to ~　～に到達する　rugby fever　ラグビーフィーバー　head coach　ヘッドコーチ（日本では「監督」）
New and Buzz Word Grand Prix　新語・流行語大賞　synonymous　同意の　nearly　ほぼ　belief　信条
［参考］次回のRugby World Cupは2023年秋にフランスで開催されるが、日本は、今回（2019年）の大会で好成績を納めたので、次回は予選を経ずして本選への出場が認められている。

Exercise 1 （ ）内に最も適切な語句を選んで、文を完成させなさい。

1. Teams from 20 countries representing ( ) of the world took part in Rugby World Cup 2019.
   (a) a region (b) some regions (c) each region
2. When the Japanese team made it to the Best 8, rugby fever spread ( ).
   (a) rapidly (b) gradually (c) slowly
3. The slogan "One Team" was proposed by the Japanese team's coach to encourage ( ).
   (a) players from abroad (b) the members of all the teams (c) all the Japanese team's players

Exercise 2 次の各文が本文の内容に合っていれば T(True)、合っていなければ F(False) と書きなさい。

____ 1. The Rugby World Cup had been held in Japan once before.
____ 2. The Japanese team played well and made it all the way to the Best 8.
____ 3. Fewer than half of the Japanese team's members were Japanese.

● Grammar Section ●

進行形

Grammar Points

動作がある時点において、進行中であることを示す動詞の形式 (be 動詞＋～ ing) を「進行形」と言います。

① They **are playing** rugby on the playground now. （現在進行形）
② An earthquake hit while we **were swimming** in the pool. （過去進行形）
③ It **will be snowing** before we get to the top of the mountain. （未来進行形）

Exercise 1 （ ）内に入る最も適切な動詞を下欄より選び、適切な動詞の形式にして空所を補いなさい。

1. While I ( ) a bath, I had a telephone call from one of my friends.
2. Some girls ( ) hard now for their dance recital.
3. We ( ) over the Pacific Ocean about this time tomorrow.

practice	fly	take

Exercise 2 （ ）内に入る適切な語句を選びなさい。

1. My sister (belongs / is belonging) to the volleyball club.
2. Please be quiet! I (study / am studying) for the history test.
3. Please wait here until my mother (comes / will come) home.

● Writing Section ●

「スポーツ」に関わる表現

Exercise 1 下の語群から適当な語を選んで、文を完成させなさい。

1. The basketball team is (   ) new members.
2. Kendo is a (   ) sport in Japan.
3. My sister is a well-known ski (   ) all around the world.

jumper	recruiting	traditional

Exercise 2 ( ) 内の語を並べかえて英文を完成させなさい。

1. 水泳は夏の最も人気のあるスポーツです。(popular / the / sport / in / most)
   Swimming is ________________________________ summer.
2. 大学ではどんなスポーツクラブに入っていますか。(to / in/ belong / you / do)
   What sports club ________________________________ college?
3. ボクシングのテレビ観戦は私には良い気晴らしになります。(a / on / favorite / TV / is)
   Watching boxing matches ____________________________ pastime of mine.

Exercise 3 日本文を英語に直しなさい。

次の "Rugby World Cup 2023" はフランスで 2023 年の秋に開催されます。

____

● Speaking Section ●

「確認」の表現

25

Exercise 1 強く発音するところの○を黒く塗りつぶしなさい。次に CD を聞いてリピートし、英文を覚えなさい。

1. A: I'm interested in playing darts. Tell me how to play. **All right?**
   ○ ○ ○ ○ ○ ○ ○ ○ ○ ○ ○ ○
   B: Sure. It's quite simple. First of all, you hold a dart like this.
   ○ ○ ○ ○ ○ ○ ○ ○ ○ ○ ○ ○ ○
2. A: I hear that you're good at dancing. **Is that true?**
   ○ ○ ○ ○ ○ ○ ○ ○ ○ ○
   B: Yes, it is. I have been learning to dance since I was a child.
   ○ ○○ ○ ○ ○ ○ ○ ○ ○ ○ ○ ○ ○

Exercise 2 日本語を参考にして、英語で言ってみましょう。

1. A: ダーツに興味があるんだけど、その遊び方を教えてよ。いいですか。
   B: いいですよ。簡単なことだから。まず、投げ矢をこのように握るのです。
2. A: ダンスがお上手だと聞いているのですけど。本当ですか。
   B: そのとおりです。ダンスは子供のころから習っています。

Exercise 3 Exercise 1 の会話をペアで練習しなさい。

Unit 5 Love and Marriage

● Listening Section ●

26

Listening Points

消える音に慣れる (2) —good day はどう聞こえる？—

[p] [t] [k] [b] [d] [g] の音が、1つ目の単語の語末と2つ目の単語の語頭の両方に現れる場合、1つ目の語末の子音の音が聞こえにくくなることがあります。例えば good day は、good の [d] の音が聞こえにくくなり、「グッディ」のように聞こえることがあります。

1. stop payment　2. what time　3. book case　4. something good
5. hot dog　6. white cap　7. good boy

Exercise 1 CD を聞いて、絵について正しく描写している英文を選びなさい。 27

1. (a) (b) (c)

2. (a) (b) (c)

Exercise 2 CD を聞いて、質問に対する最も適切な応答を選びなさい。 28

1. (a) No, it was terrible.　(b) Yes, just last night.　(c) It sounds like fun.
2. (a) That would be great.　(b) I didn't take it.　(c) I like her.

Exercise 3 CD を聞いて、次の設問に答えなさい。 29

1. Where did the man meet Mary?
   (a) At a party.
   (b) Through a university club.
   (c) At a concert.

2. What are the man's and Mary's common interests?
   (a) Music, sports, and books.
   (b) Music, travel, and sports.
   (c) Sports, reading, and art.

● Reading Section ●

Love and Marriage

Words & Phrases 次の語句の日本語訳を選びなさい。

1. increase ( ) 2. recent ( ) 3. patience ( ) 4. waste ( )
5. efficient ( ) 6. quality ( ) 7. condition ( ) 8. concern ( )
9. method ( ) 10. courage ( )

(a) 方法 (b) 条件 (c) 増加する (d) 効率的な (e) 質
(f) 懸念 (g) 浪費 (h) 最近の (i) 勇気 (j) 忍耐

30

Reading Passage

Have you ever thought of getting married? Would you like to have a life partner? The rate of unmarried people is increasing. A recent study shows that more than 50% of men and 34% of women in their late 20s have never married—or even gone out on a date. Why? Some of the people say that marriage and family life require too much money and patience. **Others say that they haven't met the right person yet.**

How can young people meet a partner? One way is through matchmaking parties. But joining a matchmaking party can be a waste of time, as you cannot always meet someone you like. The number of people who use matchmaking apps is also increasing. Matchmaking apps are efficient for finding a partner because all you have to do is click on your hoped-for qualities and conditions. There is some concern about the safety of this method, though. DNA matchmaking is a new way of matching couples that depends on people's biological compatibility. Regardless of how you meet someone, you often need courage to get married.

(184 words)

20s 20代 matchmaking parties 婚活パーティ apps (applications) アプリ hoped-for 望ましい、願った
depend on ~ ~に応じて biological compatibility 生物学的（遺伝的）な相性
Regardless of how you meet someone 出会い方のいかんを問わず

Exercise 1 本文の内容に合うように（ ）内に最も適切な語句を選んで、文を完成させなさい。

1. You need (   ) to get married and have a family.
   (a) work   (b) education   (c) patience
2. Using matchmaking apps is (   ) way to find a partner.
   (a) a bad   (b) an efficient   (c) a traditional
3. People might need (   ) to get married.
   (a) courage   (b) freedom   (c) luck

Exercise 2 次の各文が本文の内容に合っていれば T(True)、合っていなければ F(False) と書きなさい。

_____ 1. More and more people these days want to get married and have a family.

_____ 2. Matchmaking parties are good because you can always be sure you will meet the right person.

_____ 3. There is some concern about the safety of using matchmaking apps.

● Grammar Section ●

完了形

Grammar Points

完了形「have/has/had+ 過去分詞」は、時間軸上のある時点までの動作の完了、継続、経験を表します。

過去　　　　現在　　　　未来

⟶⟶（過去完了）　⟶⟶（現在完了）　⟶⟶（未来完了）

① Spring **has come**. 春が訪れました。（現在完了・完了）

② He **had** never **seen** such beautiful scenery before he came here. 彼はここに来るまでこのような美しい景色は見たことがありませんでした。（過去完了・経験）

③ I **will have been** married for five years next month. 私は来月で結婚して 5 年になります。（未来完了・継続）

Exercise 1 （ ）内に入る最も適切な語（句）を選びなさい。

1. I (will have / have / must have) been in a long-distance relationship for two years.
2. The matchmaking app (is / was / has been) popular since it first appeared.
3. I (will have / have / had) never fallen in love with anyone before I met you.

Exercise 2 次の（ ）内に適切な語を入れなさい。

1. We (   ) been good friends until that time.
2. I (   ) been sad ever since my girlfriend and I broke up.
3. By the time I arrive there, she will (   ) read the love letter I sent her.

● Writing Section ●

「恋愛・結婚」に関わる表現

Exercise 1 下の語群から適当な語（句）を選んで、文を完成させなさい。

1. Have you gotten over your (　　　　　　　　) yet?
2. It's been a long time since I saw you last. I (　　　　　　　　) you a lot.
3. Have you ever fallen in love (　　　　　　　　)?

at first sight	break-up	miss

Exercise 2 （　）内の語を並べかえて英文を完成させなさい。

1. 私たちはすでに仲直りしました。（ made / have / up ）
   We ______________________________ already.
2. もう５年彼女がいないのです。（ had / not / have ）
   I ______________________________ a girlfriend for five years.
3. 聞くところによると、リサがトムと付き合い始めたそうです。（ started / has / dating ）
   I hear Lisa ______________________________ Tom.

Exercise 3 日本文を英語に直しなさい。

中には結婚にふさわしい相手にまだ出会ったことがないと言う人がいます。（結婚に　to marry）

____

● Speaking Section ●

「ほめ言葉・感謝」の表現

31

Exercise 1 強く発音するところの○を黒く塗りつぶしなさい。次に CD を聞いてリピートし、英文を覚えなさい。

1. A: I like your jacket. **It looks good on you.**
   ○○ ○ ○ ○ ○ ○ ○ ○

   B: **Thank you**. My boyfriend gave it to me.
   ○ ○ ○ ○ ○ ○ ○ ○

2. A: Here is a present for you. I hope you like it.
   ○ ○ ○ ○ ○ ○ ○ ○ ○ ○ ○

   B: **This is so nice. I love it. Thank you so much.**
   ○○ ○ ○ ○○ ○ ○ ○ ○ ○

Exercise 2 日本語を参考にして、英語で言ってみましょう。

1. A: あなたのジャケット素敵だね。よく似合っているよ。
   B: ありがとう。彼がくれたの。
2. A: プレゼントをどうぞ。気に入ってくれるといいけど。
   B: すごく素敵。とても気に入ったわ。本当にありがとう。

Exercise 3 Exercise 1 の会話をペアで練習しなさい。

Unit 6 Weather (Typhoons)

● Listening Section ●

32

Listening Points

消える音に慣れる (3) —call her はどう聞こえる？—

くだけた会話などでは、[h] の音は聞こえなくなることがあります。たとえば、call her は「コール　ハー」ではなく、「コーラー」のように聞こえます。

1. Call her Ms. Johnson.
2. Send him this letter.
3. Tell her I'm at home.
4. Ask him this question.

Exercise 1 CD を聞いて、絵について正しく描写している英文を選びなさい。 33

1. (a) (b) (c)

2. (a) (b) (c)

Exercise 2 CD を聞いて、質問に対する最も適切な応答を選びなさい。 34

1. (a) No. I'll buy a new one tomorrow.
   (b) Only if it rains.
   (c) Yes, I do. I have one in my backpack.

2. (a) Not again!　(b) I'll check the weather report.　(c) I can hear it, too.

Exercise 3 CD を聞いて、次の設問に答えなさい。 35

1. What comes in the middle of the rainy season?
   (a) Spring warmth.
   (b) Summer heat.
   (c) Autumn coolness.

2. What happens along with heavy rainfall and thunder storms towards the end of the rainy season?
   (a) Morning sunshine.
   (b) Evening showers.
   (c) Cool evenings.

● Reading Section ●

Typhoons

Words & Phrases 次の語句の日本語訳を選びなさい。

1. suffer ( ) 2. damage ( ) 3. amount ( ) 4. district ( )
5. characterize ( ) 6. land ( ) 7. describe ( ) 8. approach ( )
9. disaster ( ) 10. minimize ( )

(a) 地方 (b) 特徴づける (c) 被害 (d) 災害 (e) 量〔額〕
(f) 接近する (g) 最小限にする (h) 描写する (i) こうむる (j) 上陸する

36

Reading Passage

Have you ever suffered serious damage from a typhoon? Every year, typhoons cause a large amount of damage somewhere in Japan. Much of it comes in what is known as "Typhoon Ginza." This is a part of Japan that typhoons most often pass through and refers mainly to Okinawa, Kyushu, Shikoku, and the southern part of Kinki district.

A typhoon is a tropical cyclone that forms near the Equator and carries strong winds, with an average wind speed of 17 meters per second or even higher. On average, 25 typhoons occur each year, and five or six of them land in Japan. Typhoons have been known throughout Japanese history. They are described as "nowaki" in several works of Japanese literature, including *The Tale of Genji* and *The Pillow Book*.

After a typhoon forms near the Equator, it takes about a week before it moves northward and approaches Japan. As a natural disaster, this makes them quite easy to forecast and prepare for. Careful preparation is the key to minimizing damage from a typhoon. So be prepared, and you will have little to worry about.

(184 words)

Typhoon Ginza 台風銀座 refer to~ ～に当てはまる tropical cyclone 熱帯低気圧 the Equator 赤道
The Tale of Genji 源氏物語 *The Pillow Book* 枕草子 nowaki 野分 minimize 最小限にする
careful preparation 念入りな準備

Exercise 1 (　) 内に最も適切な語句を選んで、文を完成させなさい。

1. The (　　　　　　　　) part of the Kinki district is included in "Typhoon Ginza."
   (a) northern　　(b) western　　(c) southern
2. A typhoon is a tropical cyclone that occurs (　　　　　　　　) the Equator.
   (a) near　　(b) on　　(c) above
3. The average number of typhoons that land in Japan every year is (　　　　　　).
   (a) 17　　(b) 25　　(c) 5 or 6

Exercise 2 次の各文が本文の内容に合っていれば T(True)、合っていなければ F(False) と書きなさい。

____ 1. Typhoons have been known in Japan for much of its history.
____ 2. After a typhoon forms, it takes about a week to reach Japan.
____ 3. Among natural disasters, typhoons are not so difficult to prepare for.

● Grammar Section ●

助動詞

Grammar Points

助動詞は動詞と結びついて、様々の意味を付け加えることができます。

① She **can** speak French.	彼女はフランス語が話**せます。**	(能力)
② You **can't** eat in the library.	図書館では食事は**できません。**	(許可)
③ It **may** rain in the afternoon.	午後は雨になる**かもしれません。**	(推量)
④ **May** I go home?	帰宅して**よろしいですか。**	(許可)
⑤ You **must** study harder.	もっと勉強しなくては**なりません。**	(義務)
⑥ You **must not** fish here.	ここで釣りをしては**いけません。**	(禁止)

Exercise 1 (　) 内に入る最も適切な語を選びなさい。

1. "(Can / Do) I wash my hands?" "Sure. This way, please."
2. "(Must / May) I borrow your pen?" "Of course. Here you go."
3. You (must / will) not leave home until you finish your homework.

Exercise 2 (　) 内に入る最も適切な助動詞を答えなさい。

1. They are waiting for you. You should get there as soon as you (　　　　　　).
2. You (　　　　　　) keep to the right when you drive in the United States.
3. "The doorbell is ringing. Would someone please answer it?"
   "Ok, I (　　　　　　) get it."

● Writing Section ●

「気象」に関わる表現

Exercise 1 下の語群から最も適当な語を選んで、文を完成させなさい。

1. The ( ) cleared when the sun rose.
2. Some bridges were washed away by the ( ).
3. Did you hear that ( )? It's going to start raining soon.

flood	snow	thunder	fog

Exercise 2 ( )内の語(句)を並べかえて英文を完成させなさい。

1. 日本は四季に恵まれています。(in / seasons / four)
   We enjoy ________________________________ Japan.
2. フロリダの夏はとても湿気が多い。(humid / in / very)
   Florida is ________________________________ the summer.
3. この空模様では一雨来そうだ。(the sky / of / the / look)
   From ________________________________, we are going to have a shower.

Exercise 3 日本文を英語に直しなさい。

大抵の台風は発生から日本接近まで 1 週間ほどかかります。

____

● Speaking Section ●

「あいづち」の表現

37

Exercise 1 強く発音するところの○を黒く塗りつぶしなさい。次に CD を聞いてリピートし、英文を覚えなさい。

1. A: I hear a big typhoon is approaching. We'd better go home as soon as possible.
   ○ ○ ○ ○ ○ ○ ○ ○ ○ ○ ○ ○ ○ ○ ○

   B: **You're right.** We'll be in trouble if the railroad service is suspended.
   ○ ○ ○ ○○ ○ ○ ○ ○ ○ ○ ○

2. A: During the rainy season, it can be very difficult to do anything outdoors.
   ○ ○ ○ ○ ○ ○ ○ ○ ○ ○ ○○ ○

   B: **I know!** It's not raining now. Shall we go to the park?
   ○ ○ ○ ○ ○ ○ ○ ○ ○ ○ ○ ○

Exercise 2 日本語を参考にして、英語で言ってみましょう。

1. A: 大型台風が接近中と聞いております。できる限り急いで帰宅した方がよいですよ。
   B: 仰る通りです。電車が不通にでもなれば、困りますからね。
2. A: 梅雨の時期には、戸外ではどのような活動も難しいですね。
   B: 分かっていますよ。今は雨が止んでいますね。公園に行きましょうか。

Exercise 3 Exercise 1 の会話をペアで練習しなさい。

Unit 7 Tourism

● Listening Section ●

38

Listening Points

消える音に慣れる（4）—R & B はどう聞こえる？—

R & B の and のように、d の直後に子音で始まる語が続くと、d の部分の空気の流れが開放されず、直後の子音がすぐに発音されるために d の部分が聞こえづらくなります。そのため、and は、「アン」のようにしか聞こえません。rock and roll のように and で結ぶ語が慣用句になると曖昧母音の a の部分も脱落して rock'n'roll のように発音も綴りも変化することもあります。

1. R & B　2. black and white　3. bread and butter　4. rock'n'roll　5. fish'n'chips

Exercise 1 CD を聞いて、絵について正しく描写している英文を選びなさい。 39

1. (a)　(b)　(c)

2. (a)　(b)　(c)

Exercise 2 CD を聞いて、質問に対する最も適切な応答を選びなさい。 40

1. (a) Yes, you can.　(b) Can I help you?　(c) Could you help me with this form?

2. (a) Let me show you on this map.
   (b) The Skytree is the tallest tower in Japan.
   (c) This kind of tree is very common here.

Exercise 3 CD を聞いて、次の設問に答えなさい。 41

1. What is the man doing?
   (a) Taking notes.
   (b) Writing a letter.
   (c) Sending a New Year's card.

2. What does the man want to thank his host family for?
   (a) Taking him to a Japanese restaurant.
   (b) Showing him around some popular tourist spots.
   (c) All of the above.

● Reading Section ●

Omotenashi, or Hospitality to Inbound Tourists

Words & Phrases 次の語句の日本語訳を選びなさい。

1. destination ( ) 2. inbound ( ) 3. attraction ( ) 4. challenge ( )
5. urgent ( ) 6. lodging ( ) 7. barrier ( ) 8. emergency ( )
9. hospitality ( ) 10. courtesy ( )

(a) 礼儀 (b) 歓待 (c) 緊急の (d) 宿泊施設 (e) 目的地
(f) 障壁 (g) 課題 (h) 海外から入ってくる (i) 引き付けるもの (j) 緊急事態

42

Reading Passage

The Japan Tourism Agency (JTA) was established in 2008. Since then, we have been working hard to make Japan an internationally attractive tourist destination. We would like more and more inbound travelers to visit Japan's many popular tourist spots and to appreciate their unique attractions.

But **there are many challenges involved in welcoming inbound visitors and making them feel at home.** The most urgent is meeting the demand for comfortable and affordable lodgings in and around tourist destinations. Another is getting over language barriers. Fortunately, more and more public places such as airports and train stations are providing multilingual announcements. Still, information for foreigners in times of emergency may not be enough. And do people on the street always give a helping hand to tourists in need of support?

The Japanese service industry is well known for offering *omotenashi*, or hospitality and courtesy, to customers and guests. Just as important is getting across our heartfelt, welcoming *omotenashi* message to inbound tourists.

(195 words)

attractive 魅力的な popular 人気のある appreciate~ ～の良さを理解する meet the demand 需要を満たす
get over ~ ～を乗り越える mutltilingual 多言語の in need of~ ～を必要としている support 支援
get across ~ ～を伝える heartfelt 心からの

Exercise 1 (　) 内に最も適切な語句を選んで、文を完成させなさい。

1. The JTA was established to promote (　　　　　　　　).
   (a) tourism　(b) cultural exchanges　(c) globalism
2. The Japanese tourism industry hopes to welcome more (　　　　　　　　) visitors.
   (a) Japanese　(b) overseas　(c) elderly
3. It is urgently important to increase the number of (　　　　　　) for foreign travelers.
   (a) lodgings　(b) tour guides　(c) tourist attractions

Exercise 2 次の各文が本文の内容に合っていれば T(True)、合っていなければ F(False) と書きなさい。

____ 1. Japanese people are famous for giving a helping hand on the street to foreigners.
____ 2. Most public places still give announcements only in Japanese.
____ 3. *Omotenashi* can be translated as hospitality and courtesy.

● Grammar Section ●

不定詞

Grammar Points

不定詞は to + 動詞の原形で、名詞的・形容詞的・副詞的用法があります。

1. 名詞的用法：　名詞の役割を担い、主語や目的語の働きがあります。「～すること」
   To exercise is important.「運動することは」 I want to study abroad.「留学することを」
2. 形容詞的用法：　名詞の直後から名詞を修飾します。「～するための」
   books to read「読むべき本」 something to eat「何か食べる物」
3. 副詞的用法：　述語全体を修飾します。目的 「～するために」 原因「～して」
   I am studying English (in order) to study abroad someday.「留学するために」
   Glad to hear that.「それを聞いて」

Exercise 1 (　) 内に入る最も適切な語 (句) を選びなさい。

1. I am going (entertain / entertaining / to entertain) some guests from Sweden today.
2. I am pleased (meet / meeting / to meet) you.
3. You're not allowed (use / using / to use) a flash in here.

Exercise 2 (　) 内の動詞を適切な形に変えて文を完成させなさい。

1. I want you (help) me with the shopping.
   ____
2. How long does it take (get) to the museum from here?
   ____
3. Where can I get something hot (drink)?
   ____

● Writing Section ●

「観光」に関わる表現

Exercise 1 下の語群から適当な語(句)を選び、文を完成させなさい。

1. Is it all right to (   ) photographs in the museum?
2. Do you happen to know how to (   ) the castle?
3. This guidebook shows where to (   ) traditional Japanese dishes.

take	try	get to

Exercise 2 ( )内の語を並べかえて英文を完成させなさい。

1. 1.　海外からの客はくつろぐように言われました。(to / make / told)
   The foreign guests were ________________________________ themselves at home.
2. 日本を訪れたのは今回が初めてですか。(to / you / visit)
   Is this the first time for ________________________________ Japan?
3. 日本家屋に入る前には靴を脱ぐことになっています。(take / to / supposed)
   You are ________________________________ off your shoes before you enter a Japanese house.

Exercise 3 日本文を英語に直しなさい。

外国からのお客様にくつろいでもらうために私たちができることがたくさんあります。

____

● Speaking Section ●

「計画・希望」の表現

43

Exercise 1 強く発音するところの○を黒く塗りつぶしなさい。次に CD を聞いてリピートし、英文を覚えなさい。

1. A: What **are you planning to** do next summer?
   ○ ○ ○ ○ ○ ○ ○ ○
   B: **I'm going to** tour around Hokkaido by bicycle.
   ○ ○ ○ ○ ○ ○ ○ ○
2. A: Where **would you like to** live, in a dorm or off campus?
   ○ ○ ○ ○ ○ ○ ○ ○ ○ ○ ○ ○
   B: I haven't decided yet, but **I hope to** share a room with somebody.
   ○ ○ ○ ○ ○ ○ ○ ○ ○ ○ ○ ○ ○

Exercise 2 日本語を参考にして、英語で言ってみましょう。

1. A: 今度の夏、どんなことを計画していますか。
   B: 自転車で北海道巡りをするつもりです。
2. A: 寮かキャンパスの外か、どちらに住みたいですか。
   B: まだ決めていませんが、誰かと相部屋を希望しています。

Exercise 3 Exercise 1 の会話をペアで練習しなさい。

Unit 8 Social Issues

● Listening Section ●

44

Listening Points

つながる音に慣れる（1）—break up はどう聞こえる？—

break up のように子音で終わる語の直後に母音で始まる語が続くと、子音と母音の連結が起こります。そのため、break と up の単語の切れ目がわかりにくくなり、「ブレイカップ」のように、まるで1語のように聞こえることがあります。

1. break up　2. come in　3. drop out　4. put on　5. Neither did I.

Exercise 1 CD を聞いて、絵について正しく描写している英文を選びなさい。

45

1. (a) (b) (c)

2. (a) (b) (c)

Exercise 2 CD を聞いて、質問に対する最も適切な応答を選びなさい。

46

1. (a) I'd be happy to.　(b) No, thank you.　(c) I'm full.
2. (a) Pretty hard.　(b) Over two hours.　(c) I'll let you know.

Exercise 3 CD を聞いて、次の設問に答えなさい。

47

1. What does the woman want to look for?
   (a) A volunteer activity.
   (b) A new job.
   (c) A daycare center.
2. Who are the speakers?
   (a) Two co-workers.
   (b) A husband and wife.
   (c) A mother and daughter.

● Reading Section ●

A Way to Tackle Clothing Loss

Words & Phrases 次の語句の日本語訳を選びなさい。

1. burn up ( )　2. on purpose ( )　3. practice ( )　4. scrap ( )
5. unsold ( )　6. maintain ( )　7. worldwide ( )　8. tackle ( )
9. totally ( )　10. original ( )

(a) 焼き払う　(b) 維持する　(c) 廃棄する　(d) 故意に　(e) 全く
(f) 取り組む　(g) 売れ残った　(h) 元の　(i) 世界中で　(j) 慣習

48

Reading Passage

A certain British fashion company recently burned up four billion yen worth of new clothing—and they did it on purpose! Why would they do such a thing? To make a long story short, the company wanted to avoid selling their products at a reduced price. In the fashion industry, it has long been a common practice to scrap unsold new clothing as a way to protect the maker's brand image. The British company was, however, severely criticized as being wasteful and "environmentally unfriendly."

So, **what is important for fashion companies these days is to maintain their brand image** and to protect the environment at the same time. But how? Various efforts are being made worldwide to tackle this problem.

Let me tell you about how one Japanese company is dealing with the issue. First, it purchases unsold new clothes from stores that sell high-fashion brands. Then the company changes the brand labels to make the items look like the fashions of a totally different (and less "fashionable") brand. Lastly, the company sells the goods cheaply online. The brand image isn't harmed because the name of the original high-class brand is never shown. What a great idea!

(197 words)

clothing loss 衣料品ロス(売れ残った新品の衣料品が未販売のまま廃棄されること。)　certain ~ ある~(限定詞的用法)
four billion yen worth of ~ 40 億円に相当する~　at a reduced price 割引き値段で　environmentally 環境的に
effort 試み　brand label ブランドタグ

Exercise 1 (　) 内に最も適切な語を選んで、文を完成させなさい。

1. People criticized the British company's scrapping of unsold new clothes as (　　　　　　　).
   (a) environmental　(b) wasteful　(c) thoughtful
2. It is (　　　　　　　) for companies to protect both their brand image and the environment.
   (a) able　(b) unable　(c) important
3. The Japanese company sells the clothes cheaply online by changing the original (　　　　　　　).
   (a) sizes　(b) labels　(c) designs

Exercise 2 次の各文が本文の内容に合っていれば T(True)、合っていなければ F(False) と書きなさい。

_____ 1. The British fashion company wanted to sell off its clothes at bargain prices.
_____ 2. The scrapping of unsold new clothing has never been a common practice.
_____ 3. The Japanese company does not give out the original brand name.

● Grammar Section ●

動名詞

Grammar Points

1. 動名詞は動詞の ing 形で表され、通常「～すること」と訳されて、名詞の働きをします。
   Playing tennis is fun.　テニスをすることは楽しい。
2. enjoy, give up, avoid, finish, mind, practice は、目的語として不定詞ではなく動名詞をとります。
   I enjoyed **talking** with you.　一緒に話をして楽しかったです。
3. remember, forget, regret は、目的語が不定詞か動名詞かで意味が異なります。
   Remember to post the letter.　忘れずに手紙を投函してください。
   I remember **posting** the letter.　手紙を投函したことを覚えています。

Exercise 1 (　) 内に入る最も適切な語 (句) を選びなさい。

1. I gave up (to drink / drinking / drank) after the accident.
2. It took me a long time to get used to (live / living / have lived) in Rome.
3. The homeless man died after (leave / leaving / left) the hospital.

Exercise 2 (　) 内の動詞を動名詞に変えて文を完成させなさい。

1. I want to avoid (shop) on the Internet. ____________
2. I shall never forget (meet) the movie star in person. ____________
3. The doctor was stressed out because of (have) too much work. ____________

● Writing Section ●

「社会問題」に関わる表現

Exercise 1 下の語群から適語を選び、適切な形に変えて文を完成させなさい。

1. (　　　　　　　　　) has been shown to cause cancer.
2. (　　　　　　　　　) a job these days is not easy.
3. Thank you for (　　　　　　　　　) the police.

call	find	smoke

Exercise 2 (　) 内の語を並べかえて英文を完成させなさい。

1. 私は近所の騒音について不平を言うのをやめました。(complaining / the / about)
   I stopped ______________________________ noise from my neighbor.
2. あなたの離婚について尋ねてもよろしいですか。(asking / about / my)
   Do you mind ______________________________ your divorce?
3. 私はレポートに日本の社会制度について書こうと思っています。(thinking / writing / of)
   For my report, I am ______________________________ about Japan's social system.

Exercise 3 日本文を英語に直しなさい。

大切なことは、毎日練習を続けることです。(練習を続ける keep practicing)

____

● Speaking Section ●

「注意・許可」の表現

49

Exercise 1 強く発音するところの○を黒く塗りつぶしなさい。次に CD を聞いてリピートし、英文を覚えなさい。

1. A: Mom, may I go to the beach with my friends next week?
   ○ ○○○○ ○ ○ ○ ○○ ○ ○

   B: **Yes**, of course. But **be careful not to** get sunburned.
   ○ ○ ○ ○ ○ ○ ○ ○ ○ ○

2. A: I'm having a problem with my computer. Do you mind if I use yours?
   ○ ○ ○ ○ ○ ○ ○ ○ ○ ○ ○○○ ○

   B: **No, not at all**. You are welcome to use it anytime.
   ○ ○○○ ○○ ○ ○○ ○○

Exercise 2 日本語を参考にして、英語で言ってみましょう。

1. A: お母さん、来週友達と海水浴場に行ってもいいかな。
   B: いいわよ、もちろん。でも、日焼けしないようにね。
2. A: パソコンの調子が悪いの。あなたのパソコンを借りてもいいかな。
   B: ええ、かまわないよ。いつでも使ってね。

Exercise 3 Exercise 1 の会話をペアで練習しなさい。

Unit 9 Study Skills

● Listening Section ●

50

Listening Points

つながる音に慣れる（2）—an egg はどう聞こえる？—

an egg のように [n] の直後に母音で始まる語が続くと、子音と母音の連結が起こります。そのため、an と egg の単語の切れ目がわかりにくくなり、「アネッグ」のように、まるで1語のように聞こえることがあります。

1. an apple　2. an orange　3. an engineer　4. in an hour　5. seven o' clock

6. Give me an example.　7. Can I get you something to drink?

Exercise 1 CD を聞いて、絵について正しく描写している英文を選びなさい。 51

1.　(a)　(b)　(c)

2.　(a)　(b)　(c)

Exercise 2 CD を聞いて、質問に対する最も適切な応答を選びなさい。 52

1. (a) Mine are excellent.　(b) No skills are required for the job.　(c) No, what does that mean?

2. (a) I'll look it up for you on my computer.
   (b) You can buy one at the grocery store.
   (c) Yes, that's a difficult word.

Exercise 3 CD を聞いて、次の設問に答えなさい。 53

1. What does the woman have to do?
   (a) Study for the exam.
   (b) Listen to music.
   (c) Get a lot of information.

2. What is the man's advice?
   (a) Concentrate harder.
   (b) Turn down the music.
   (c) Study in the library.

● Reading Section ●

Study Skills

Words & Phrases 次の語句の日本語訳を選びなさい。

1. effectively (　)　2. tip (　)　3. utmost (　)　4. achieve (　)
5. motivate (　)　6. specific (　)　7. session (　)　8. decision (　)
9. constantly (　)　10. review (　)

(a) 最大限　(b) 常に　(c) 効果的に　(d) 復習する　(e) 期間
(f) コツ　(g) 具体的な　(h) 達成する　(i) 決定　(j) やる気をおこさせる

54

Reading Passage

How can we study more effectively? Here are some useful tips.

First, set a clear goal and do your utmost to achieve it. **There are two ways of keeping yourself motivated to reach your goal.** One is to actually tell your friends and family what your goal is. That way, your goal becomes a promise that you won't want to break. The other way is to keep your goal to yourself and dream about surprising everyone when you successfully reach your objective.

Second, make specific plans to achieve the goal in either of two ways. One is to cram the material to be learned into one session. For example, you could study English only on Sundays for 70 minutes without a break. The other is to break your study time up into several short sessions, e.g., seven 10-minute sessions, and repeat the material every day.

Which way is better? The decision is up to you. But my advice is that the latter is more effective because the spaced study time keeps you constantly reviewing the material you want to learn.

(186 words)

that way そうすれば　objective 目標　cram 詰め込み勉強をする　the material to be learned 学習すべき教材
without a break 中断なく　break ~ up into … ~を…に分割する　e.g., = for example, 例えば
be up to ~ ~次第である　the latter 後者

Exercise 1 (　) 内に最も適切な語句を選んで、文を完成させなさい。

1. The writer's main purpose is to help us (　　　　　　　) more effectively.
   (a) set goals　　(b) dream　　(c) study
2. If you (　　　　　　　) your goal with your friends and family, you will be motivated to try harder to achieve it.
   (a) set　　(b) reach　　(c) share
3. The writer's strongest advice is to (　　　　　　　).
   (a) cram the material to be learned into one session
   (b) spread the material over several study sessions
   (c) both (a) and (b)

Exercise 2 次の各文が本文の内容に合っていれば T(True)、合っていなければ F(False) と書きなさい。

____ 1. As the first step in developing study skills, set a clear goal.
____ 2. The writer is against keeping your goal to yourself.
____ 3. The writer believes that we should study English only on Sundays.

● Grammar Section ●

受動態

Grammar Points

受動態（受け身）とは、「～が（…により）…される」という意味を表し、be 動詞＋動詞の過去分詞の文型を取ります。行為者の情報「by ～の部分」は通常は省略されます。
感情を表す動詞はその感情を発する動作の主体を主語にして受動態で表されます。

① Various subjects **are taught** here. ここでは様々な科目が教えられています。
② The theater **was built** last year.　その劇場は去年建てられました。
③ Computers **have been used in** classrooms. コンピュータが教室で使われてきました。
④ The project **will be carried out** in the future. そのプロジェクトは将来実行されます。
⑤ We **are satisfied with** this method. 私達はこの方法に満足しています。

Exercise 1 (　) 内に入る最も適切な語 (句) を選びなさい。

1. I (am interest / am interested / am interesting) in developing better study skills.
2. Last week, the class (divides / is divided / was divided) into four groups.
3. It (says / is said / said) that 21 days are needed to form a new habit.

Exercise 2 (　) 内の語句を主語にして文を書き換えなさい。

1. We ask (students) to think about how to study more effectively.

____

2. Many schools have introduced (active learning).

____

3. We will talk about (the learner-friendly curriculum).

____

● Writing Section ●

「Study Skills」に関わる表現

Exercise 1 下の語群から適当な語を選んで、文を完成させなさい。

1. (　　　　　　　　　) skills should be acquired as a way to better understand lectures.
2. A large variety of resources such as study guides and (　　　　　　　　　　　　) are provided online.
3. The talk on how to study more (　　　　　　　　　) will be given in the lecture hall.

tutorials	note-taking	efficiently

Exercise 2 (　) 内の語を並べかえて英文を完成させなさい。

1. 効果的な勉強のスキルは様々な種類の科目に取り組む事に応用できます。(applied / can / be)
   Effective study skills ______________________________ to various kinds of subjects.
2. 勉強では何をすべきかを書き出しなさい。(done / should / be)
   Write down what ______________________________ in your study sessions.
3. 今勉強すべきことを先延ばしにしてはいけません。(what / be /should)
   Don't put off ______________________________ studied now.

Exercise 3 日本文を英語に直しなさい。

勉強する意欲を保ち続けることは重要です。

____

● Speaking Section ●

「謝罪」の表現

55

Exercise 1 強く発音するところの○を黒く塗りつぶしなさい。次に CD を聞いてリピートし、英文を覚えなさい。

1. A: **Sorry to be late.** I missed my usual train.
   ○　○ ○○　○ ○　○○　○

   B: No problem. So, let's get started.
   ○　○　○ ○　○　○

2. A: **I am terribly sorry.** I'm afraid the document is missing.
   ○○　○　○　○　○　○ ○　○　○

   B: Missing? No way! Don't let it happen again.
   ○　○ ○　○　○○ ○　○

Exercise 2 日本語を参考にして、英語で言ってみましょう。

1. A: 遅れてごめん。いつもの電車に乗り遅れたんだ。
   B: 大丈夫よ。さあ始めましょう。
2. A: 大変申し訳ありません。書類が見当たらないようで。
   B: 見当たらないって。あり得ない。二度と起こらないようにしなさい。

Exercise 3 Exercise 1 の会話をペアで練習しなさい。

Unit 10 Health and Welfare

● Listening Section ●

56

Listening Points

つながる音に慣れる（3）—clear up はどう聞こえる？—

clear up のように [r] の直後に母音で始まる語が続くと、子音と母音の連結が起こります。そのため、clear と up の単語の切れ目がわかりにくくなり、「クリアラップ」のように、まるで 1 語のように聞こえることがあります。

1. clear up　　2. for example　　3. never again　　4. clever ideas

Exercise 1 CD を聞いて、絵について正しく描写している英文を選びなさい。

57

1. (a)　(b)　(c)

2. (a)　(b)　(c)

Exercise 2 CD を聞いて、質問に対する最も適切な応答を選びなさい。

58

1. (a) I'm Bob Smith.　(b) No thanks. I already have one.　(c) Yes, I do. Here you are.
2. (a) Good idea.　(b) Yes, let's walk.　(c) No, I'll take a taxi instead.

Exercise 3 CD を聞いて、次の設問に答えなさい。

59

1. Where does this conversation take place?
   (a) At a school.
   (b) At a hospital.
   (c) In an office.
2. Who most likely is the woman?
   (a) A nurse.
   (b) A doctor.
   (c) A patient.

● Reading Section ●

"Boshi Techo" and Its Globalization

Words & Phrases 次の語句の日本語訳を選びなさい。

1. local government (　) 2. pregnant (　) 3. reduce (　) 4. death rate (　)
5. include (　) 6. health condition (　) 7. valuable (　) 8. benefits (　)
9. literacy rate (　) 10. risk (　)

(a) 識字率　(b) 利点　(c) 危険　(d) 有益な　(e) 妊娠した
(f) 地方自治体　(g) 含む　(h) 健康状態　(i) 減少させる　(j) 死亡率

60

Reading Passage

"Boshi Techo," or " The Mother and Child Health Handbook," was first given out by local governments in 1948 to all pregnant women in Japan, and it has helped to greatly reduce the death rates of new mothers and babies. "Boshi Techo" includes sections for recording of mothers' health conditions and babies' growth and vaccinations. Most importantly, it has provided valuable information on how to maintain the health of both mothers and babies.

In the early 1990s, an Indonesian doctor showed great interest in the educational benefits of the handbook, and introduced an Indonesian version of "Boshi Techo" to his country. At first, it was introduced to only one province, but now, it is found all over the country.

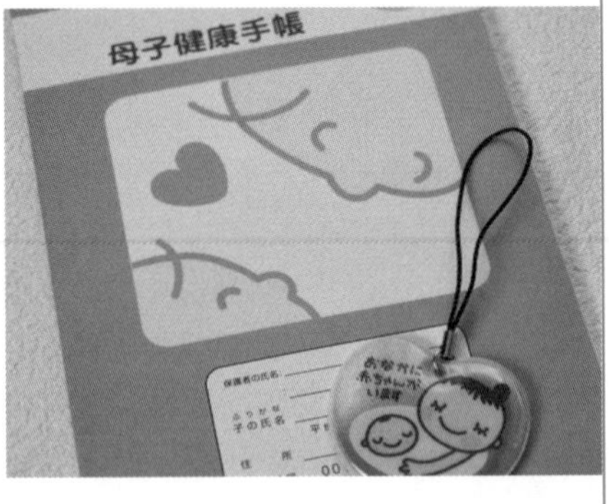

Today, **"Boshi Techo" is used in 50 countries around the world**. In some countries where the literacy rate is especially low, pictures are used so that mothers can understand the contents. The more "Boshi Techo" is used, the more women everywhere will be saved from the risks of childbirth.

(168 words)

母子健康手帳（第二次世界大戦後、栄養失調や感染症からの母子を守るために作られた手帳。「母子手帳」と呼ばれることが多い。日本に在住する外国人や英語圏の国では、"Mother and Child Health handbook" としても知られている。）　vaccination ワクチン接種　province 州、省、県など行政区分を意味する語（インドネシアの場合は「州」という日本語訳にするのが適切。）　so that ~ can... ～が…できるように　The + 比較級 , the + 比較級　～すればするほど～だ

Exercise 1 （ ）内に最も適切な語句を選んで、文を完成させなさい。

1. ( ) give "Boshi Techo" to all pregnant mothers in Japan.
   (a) Hospitals (b) Local governments (c) Doctors
2. One Indonesian doctor brought back the idea of Japan's "Boshi Techo" to his country in the ( ).
   (a) 1940s (b) 1950s (c) 1990s
3. Now, "Boshi Techo" is ( ) used all over the globe.
   (a) widely (b) possibly (c) hardly

Exercise 2 次の各文が本文の内容に合っていれば T(True)、合っていなければ F(False)と書きなさい。

____ 1. In some places, "The Mother and Child Health Handbook" has to have pictures to make it easier for mothers to use.

____ 2. Only in Japan have mothers' and babies' death rates been reduced thanks to "Boshi Techo."

____ 3. "Boshi Techo" is being used outside Japan to help decrease the risks of childbirth.

● Grammar Section ●

前置詞

Grammar Points

前置詞は、場所や時間、または範囲などを表す表現の前に置かれます。例えば in は広い範囲の場所や時間を表す表現の前に置かれますが、on はやや狭く、at はもっと狭い範囲の時に使われます。また、by と until の前置詞の使い分けにも注意しましょう。

① I visited Rome **in** 2019. / I live **in** Kyoto.
② Are you busy **on** Sunday ? / The bank is **on** King Street.
③ The shop opens **at** 10 a.m. / Let's meet **at** the front desk later.
④ The meeting lasts **until** 5 p.m. / He'll come back to work **by** the end **of** this week.

Exercise 1 （ ）内に入る最も適切な語を選びなさい。

1. There are lots of exercise machines (in / on / at) this room.
2. The hospital is (in / on / by) the corner of King St. and Flanders St.
3. Patients are to submit this form (by / until / in) May 15th.

Exercise 2 （ ）内に適切な前置詞を入れなさい。

1. There is an interdependent relationship ( ) nurses and physicians.
2. The family doctor was in New York ( ) January.
3. We didn't notice the symptoms of the disease ( ) that time.

● Writing Section ●

「保健・福祉」に関わる表現

Exercise 1 下の語群から適当な語を選んで、文を完成させなさい。

1. How about going (　　　　) a walk?
2. We worked out (　　　　) the gym last night.
3. The doctor asked me to come back (　　　　) one week.

at	for	in

Exercise 2 (　) 内の語を並べかえて英文を完成させなさい。

1. 私は喫煙に反対です。(against / am / smoking)
   I ____.
2. 保健所はちょうど角をまがったところにあります。(the / corner / around)
   The health care center is just ______________________________.
3. 私の祖父は昨日入院しました。(was / to / admitted)
   My grandfather ______________________________ a hospital yesterday.

Exercise 3 日本文を英語に直しなさい。

その新しい薬は、今この病院で使われています。

____

● Speaking Section ●

「提案・同意」の表現

61

Exercise 1 強く発音するところの○を黒く塗りつぶしなさい。次に CD を聞いてリピートし、英文を覚えなさい。

1. A: I love the muffins from that coffee shop over there.
   ○○ ○ ○ ○ ○ ○ ○ ○ ○
   B: **Same here.** If you have time now, **shall we** go have some?
   ○ ○ ○ ○ ○ ○ ○ ○ ○ ○ ○ ○
2. A: I didn't go to the gym last week.
   ○○ ○○ ○○ ○ ○
   B: **Neither did I.** I had to work overtime every day, from Monday to Friday.
   ○ ○○○○ ○ ○ ○ ○ ○ ○ ○ ○ ○

Exercise 2 日本語を参考にして、英語で言ってみましょう。

1. A: 私はあちらのコーヒーショップのマフィンが大好きなの。
   B: 私もだよ。もし今時間があったら、食べに行かない？
2. A: 先週はジムに行かなかったんだよ。
   B: 私もよ。月曜から金曜まで毎日残業をしないといけなくて。

Exercise 3 Exercise 1 の会話をペアで練習しなさい。

Unit 11 Environmental Issues

● Listening Section ●

62

Listening Points

変化する音に慣れる（1） —with sugar はどう聞こえる？—

with sugar において強勢を受けない with や have to / has to のようによく使われる成句などでは、[ð] の音が [θ] に、[v] の音が [f] に、[z] の音が [s] に変化することがあります。

1. with sugar [ð] → [θ]
2. have to [v] → [f]
3. of course [v] → [f]
4. has to [z] → [s]

Exercise 1 CD を聞いて、絵について正しく描写している英文を選びなさい。

63

1. (a) (b) (c)

2. (a) (b) (c)

Exercise 2 CD を聞いて、質問に対する最も適切な応答を選びなさい。

64

1. (a) It's a little cloudy. (b) I heard it on the news. (c) Let's go out for a run.
2. (a) Let me help you. (b) As much as I can. (c) I don't have a bicycle.

Exercise 3 CD を聞いて、次の設問に答えなさい。

65

1. Which of these is NOT included in the 3Rs?
   (a) Reuse.
   (b) Reduce.
   (c) Recover.
2. What does the woman think of the 3Rs?
   (a) She has no idea what it means.
   (b) She thinks the idea is silly.
   (c) She thinks the 3Rs are necessary for saving the Earth.

● Reading Section ●

Coffee Crisis

Words & Phrases 次の語句の日本語訳を選びなさい。

1. reasonable ( ) 2. consumption ( ) 3. production ( )
4. global warming ( ) 5. suitable ( ) 6. develop ( )
7. affect ( ) 8. resistant ( ) 9. support ( ) 10. regret ( )

(a) 生産 (b) 消費 (c) 開発する (d) 手ごろな (e) 適した
(f) 耐性がある (g) 支援する (h) 地球温暖化 (i) 後悔する (j) 影響を与える

66

Reading Passage

Coffee is a popular drink. Coffee shops are found all around the world. In Japan, we can buy a delicious cup of coffee for just 100 yen at convenience stores. Soon, however, it might become difficult to enjoy good coffee at a reasonable price. There are two reasons for this.

First, the consumption of coffee is increasing so rapidly that coffee bean production cannot keep up with it. Second, coffee beans are grown in areas with both rainy and dry seasons. In addition, the days should be hot and the nights quite cold. Because of global warming, however, weather patterns are changing. There is less land that is suitable for growing coffee.

Various efforts are being made to find solutions. Starbucks has begun developing coffee beans that are not easily affected by climate change. It is giving the beans to coffee growers for free. Japan's best-known coffee company is collecting coffee seedlings and studying them to see which are the most resistant to global warming. **We should do what we can to support coffee growers and coffee bean production.** Otherwise, when our favorite drink disappears, we will surely regret it.

(190 words)

delicious おいしい　rapidly 急速に　keep up with ~ ～に遅れないでついていく　weather 天候　solution 解決策
climate change 気候変動　for free 無料で　seedling 苗木　study ~ ～を研究する　otherwise さもなければ
disappear 姿を消す

Exercise 1 (　) 内に最も適切な語句を選んで、文を完成させなさい。

1. People are drinking ( ) coffee than before.
   (a) more (b) less (c) much less
2. Coffee beans are grown in areas with ( ) temperature difference between day and night.
   (a) no (b) a small (c) a large
3. ( ) has caused coffee bean production to decrease.
   (a) Starbucks (b) Global warming (c) Japan's leading coffee company

Exercise 2 次の各文が本文の内容に合っていれば T(True)、合っていなければ F(False) と書きなさい。

_____ 1. Coffee costs about 100 yen at most coffee shops in cities worldwide.
_____ 2. Coffee bean production is greater than coffee bean consumption.
_____ 3. Starbucks is giving coffee beans that are resistant to global warming to coffee farmers.

● Grammar Section ●

接続詞

Grammar Points

接続詞には文と文、語と語など対等な関係のものをつなぐ等位接続詞と主節と従属節とをつなぐ従位接続詞があります。

・等位接続詞：and, but, or, for, so など

Mary is a teacher, **and** Emma is a doctor.　メアリーは教師で、エマは医者です。

・従位接続詞：that（～ということ）、if（～なら）、because（～なので）、when（～する時）、though（～であるけれども）など

Tell me **when** you are ready.　準備ができた時、知らせてください。

Exercise 1 (　) 内に入る接続詞を選びなさい。

1. It is hot, (but / or / so) I turned on the air conditioner.
2. Summers were cooler (if / because / when) I was a child.
3. I believe (so / that / because) global warming is the Earth's most serious problem.

Exercise 2 (　) 内に適切な接続詞を入れなさい。

1. To reduce greenhouse gasses, we should reduce, reuse, ( ) recycle wastes.
2. ( ) we don't try hard enough to prevent it, global warming will get worse.
3. We opened the window ( ) it was very hot in the room.

● Writing Section ●

「環境問題」に関わる表現

Exercise 1 下の語群から適当な語を選んで、文を完成させなさい。

1. Living in the countryside is not convenient, (　　　　　　　　　　) the air is cleaner and fresher.
2. (　　　　　　　　　) you don't turn the tap off, you will waste a lot of water.
3. I always bring my own shopping bag (　　　　　　　　　　) I want to help reduce plastic waste.

because	but	if

Exercise 2 (　) 内の語を並べかえて英文を完成させなさい。

1. 今、行動しなければ遅すぎることになってしまうでしょう。(we / if / don't)
   ______________________ act now, it'll be too late.
2. 天気予報によると今週末雪が降るようです。(said / forecast / that)
   The weather ______________________ it would snow this weekend.
3. 私は部屋を出る時、いつも電気を消します。(I / when / leave)
   ______________________ a room, I always turn off the lights.

Exercise 3 日本文を英語に直しなさい。

私たちは地球を救うためにできることをすべきです。(地球を救う save the Earth)

____

● Speaking Section ●

「依頼・承諾」の表現

67

Exercise 1 強く発音するところの○を黒く塗りつぶしなさい。次に CD を聞いてリピートし、英文を覚えなさい。

1. A: **Would you** do me a favor? I need some help.
   ○ ○ ○ ○○○ ○ ○ ○ ○
   B: **Sure**. What can I do for you?
   ○ ○ ○ ○ ○ ○ ○
2. A: **Would you mind** helping me?
   ○ ○ ○ ○ ○
   B: **Not at all**. I'd be happy to.
   ○ ○○ ○ ○ ○ ○

Exercise 2 日本語を参考にして、英語で言ってみましょう。

1. A: お願いがあるんだけど。手伝ってほしいの。
   B: もちろん。何をしたらいい？
2. A: 手伝ってくれる？
   B: もちろん。喜んで。

Exercise 3 Exercise 1 の会話をペアで練習しなさい。

Unit 12 Languages

● Listening Section ●

68

Listening Points

変化する音に慣れる（2） —did you はどう聞こえる？—

[t], [d] などの子音で終わる単語の直後に半母音 [j] の音で始まる単語が続くと、子音と半母音の連結で音変化が起こり、１つの単語のように聞こえます。

① It's nice to <u>meet you</u>. [t] + [j] → [ʧ]

② What time <u>did you</u> go to bed last night? [d] + [j] → [ʤ]

Exercise 1 CD を聞いて、絵について正しく描写している英文を選びなさい。 69

1. (a) (b) (c)

2. (a) (b) (c)

Exercise 2 CD を聞いて、質問に対する最も適切な応答を選びなさい。 70

1. (a) Yes, I can. (b) I'm learning Chinese. (c) Two.
2. (a) Yes, I did. (b) No, I won't. (c) So did I.

Exercise 3 CD を聞いて、次の設問に答えなさい。 71

1. What does Tom Smith do?
   - (a) He is a college teacher.
   - (b) He is an exchange student.
   - (c) He is a college counselor.
2. Where does the foreign student come from?
   - (a) France.
   - (b) Germany.
   - (c) Austria.

● Reading Section ●

Languages

Words & Phrases 次の語句の日本語訳を選びなさい。

1. approximately (　) 2. native speaker (　) 3. the case (　)
4. considering (　) 5. huge (　) 6. unfortunately (　)
7. endangered (　) 8. disappear (　) 9. die out (　) 10. asset (　)

(a) 危険にさらされた (b) 事実 (c) 資産 (d) 残念ながら (e) 母語話者
(f) 膨大な (g) 死滅する (h) 約、およそ (i) 考慮すると (j) 消える

72

Reading Passage

According to the latest data, approximately 7,100 languages are spoken in the world today. Does it surprise you that there are so many? It does me!

Now, let's ask ourselves what language is spoken by the most people. If you answered English, sorry, you're wrong, sort of. The correct answer is Mandarin Chinese, if, that is, we count only native speakers. It's pretty easy to see why this is the case, considering China's huge population, which is now about 1.4 billion people. But if we count both native and non-native speakers, then **the number of English speakers worldwide is the largest**, followed by Mandarin Chinese, Hindi, and Spanish.

What about languages that have fewer speakers? Well, there are lots of those around the globe, too, but unfortunately, many are endangered. In fact, some studies show that about 40 percent of all the world's languages could soon disappear. And when a language dies out, a valuable cultural asset disappears along with it. This, for many reasons, means a great loss for humanity.

(171 words)

according to ~ ～によると　latest data 最新のデータ　sort of 多少　Mandarin Chinese 標準中国語　non-native 母国ではない　be followed by ~ ～が次に続く　Hindi ヒンズー語　around the globe 世界中で　valuable cultural asset 価値のある文化的資産　great loss 大きな損失　humanity 人類

CIAO (イタリア語), 你好 (中国語), BONJOUR (フランス語) は、Hello (英語) と同意の「挨拶語」

データは外務省のホームページより

Exercise 1 (　) 内に適切な語 (句) を選んで、文を完成しなさい。

1. There are (　　　　　　　　　　) languages in the world.
   (a) exactly 7,000　　(b) more than 7,000　　(c) fewer than 7,000
2. When both native and non-native speakers are taken into account, (　　　　　　　　　　) has the most speakers worldwide.
   (a) English　　(b) Chinese　　(c) Hindi
3. Many languages are now (　　　　　　　　　　).
   (a) appearing　　(b) changing　　(c) disappearing

Exercise 2 次の各文が本文の内容に合っていれば T(True)、合っていなければ F(False) と書きなさい。

_____ 1. China's population has now reached about 1.4 million people.
_____ 2. About 40 percent of the world's languages are now in danger of dying out.
_____ 3. When one language disappears, it's no great loss to humanity.

● Grammar Section ●

比較

Grammar Points

複数のものを比べる時に以下のような「比較」の形 (原級・比較級・最上級) で表現できます。

① Tim is **as old as** Steve. (原級)
② She is **taller than** her friend. (比較級)
③ This book is **more expensive than** that one. (比較級)
④ We should speak **more slowly.** (比較級)
⑤ He is **the tallest** in his class. (最上級)
⑥ This flower is **the most beautiful** here. (最上級)
⑦ This tool is used (**the**) **most often.** (最上級)

Exercise 1 (　) 内に入る最も適切な語 (句) を選びなさい。

1. Jack learned new words (more quickly / the most quickly) than Lora.
2. English is the (most popular / popularest) foreign language in Japan.
3. I think English is (easy / easier) than German.

Exercise 2 (　) 内に適切な語を入れなさい。

1. Among college students, Chinese is often chosen as the (　　　　　　　　　　) popular second language.
2. Which is (　　　　　　　　　　) difficult to pronounce for Japanese people, French or Spanish?
3. Joy speaks English better (　　　　　　　　　　) any other student in her class.

● Writing Section ●

「言語」に関わる表現

Exercise 1 下の語群から適当な語を選んで、文を完成させなさい。

1. Reading aloud is more (   ) than memorizing vocabulary when learning a foreign language.
2. Watching videos is the (   ) way to master a foreign language.
3. She learned English more (   ) than most of her classmates.

best	easily	helpful

Exercise 2 (　) 内の語を並べかえて英文を完成させなさい。

1. 由美と英語を勉強することは１人で勉強するよりもっと楽しい。(enjoyable / is / more)

   Studying English with Yumi ______________________________ than studying by myself.

2. 私にとってリスニングはリーディングよりずっと難しい。(harder / than / much)

   For me, listening comprehension is ______________________________ reading comprehension.

3. 私はあなたと同じぐらい上手に韓国語を話すことができます。(well / as / as)

   I can speak Korean ______________________________ you can.

Exercise 3 日本文を英語に直しなさい。

スペイン語を話す人の数は世界で最も多くはありません。

____

● Speaking Section ●

「申し出・断り」の表現

73

Exercise 1 強く発音するところの○を黒く塗りつぶしなさい。次に CD を聞いてリピートし、英文を覚えなさい。

1. A: **Would you like** another cup of coffee?
   ○ ○○ ○ ○○○

   B: **No, thank you. I've had plenty.**
   ○ ○ ○○ ○ ○

2. A: **Shall I help you with** your homework?
   ○○○ ○ ○ ○ ○

   B: **Thank you, but** I had better do it on my own.
   ○ ○ ○○○ ○ ○○○ ○○

Exercise 2 日本語を参考にして、英語で言ってみましょう。

1. A: `コーヒーのおかわりはいかがですか。

   B: いいえ、結構です。十分いただきました。

2. A: 宿題を手伝いましょうか。

   B: ありがとう、でも自分でやった方がいいので。

Exercise 3 Exercise 1 の会話をペアで練習しなさい。

Unit 13 Guide to Foreign Countries

● Listening Section ●

74

Listening Points

変化する音に慣れる（3） ―miss you はどう聞こえる？―

[s], [z] などの子音で終わる単語の直後に半母音 [j] の音で始まる単語が続くと、子音と半母音の連結で音変化が起こり、1 つの単語のように聞こえます。

① It's been a long time. I <u>miss you</u> so much.　[s] + [j] → [ʃ]

② You can eat as much <u>as you</u> like.　[z] + [j] → [ʒ]

Exercise 1 CD を聞いて、絵について正しく描写している英文を選びなさい。 75

1.　(a)　(b)　(c)

2.　(a)　(b)　(c)

Exercise 2 CD を聞いて、質問に対する最も適切な応答を選びなさい。 76

1. (a) Yes, it is large.　(b) I don't know where Finland is.　(c) Helsinki is.
2. (a) Yes, once.　(b) No, not right now.　(c) Yes, I would.

Exercise 3 CD を聞いて、次の設問に答えなさい。 77

1. Where did the man once live?
   (a) In Canada.
   (b) In Denmark.
   (c) In an old castle.
2. How many times has the man been to Europe?
   (a) Only once.
   (b) A few times.
   (c) Never.

● Reading Section ●

Finland

Words & Phrases 次の語句の日本語訳を選びなさい。

1. scenery ( )　2. own ( )　3. incredibly ( )　4. temperature ( )
5. plunge ( )　6. go without saying ( )　7. frozen solid ( )　8. all day long ( )
9. by the way ( )　10. (be) located ( )

(a) 一日中　(b) 信じられないことに　(c) カチカチに凍った　(d) 位置する　(e) 景色
(f) 飛び込む　(g) 所有する　(h) 言うまでもない　(i) 気温　(j) ところで

78

Reading Passage

Hauska tavata! That's how you say "Nice to meet you" in Finnish, spoken in Finland. Finland is well known for its beautiful scenery, saunas, and, of course, Santa Claus Village.

Today, **Finland is home to around 5 million people**. It is also "home" to about 187,000 lovely lakes — one lake for every 27 people. No wonder, then, that so many Finns own a cottage on a lake, where in summer they enjoy cruising on a boat.

Finns love their saunas. Incredibly, in winter, when the temperature drops below zero, lots of people like to plunge into an ice-cold lake after they enjoy a sauna. It goes without saying that many Finnish lakes are frozen solid in winter. This means you can walk, skate or even drive your car on them.

In Lapland, in Finland's far north, the sun never appears in winter. It's dark all day long. Lapland, by the way, is where the Santa Claus Village is located. If you want, you can have your picture taken with Santa.

(171 words)

Finland is home to ~ フィンランドには～が住んでいる　No wonder, then, that ~ ですから～というのも驚くにあたりません
Lapland ノルウェー、スウェーデン、フィンランドの各北部及びロシア・コラ半島にまたがる地域の総称で大部分が北極圏内
Santa Claus Village フィンランド国内のラップランド（Lapland）地域はラッピ県（Lappi）と呼ばれ、その首都ロヴァニエミ（Rovaniemi）郊外にあるテーマパーク

Exercise 1 (　) 内に最も適切な語句を選んで、文を完成させなさい。

1. Finland has thousands of beautiful (　　　　　　　　).
   (a) rivers　　(b) lakes　　(c) homes
2. Many Finnish people enjoy (　　　　　　　　) cold lakes after being in a sauna.
   (a) jumping into　　(b) walking on　　(c) staying beside
3. In (　　　　　　　　), the sun doesn't rise in the the north of Finland.
   (a) September　　(b) July　　(c) December

Exercise 2 次の各文が本文の内容に合っていれば T(True)、合っていなければ F(False) と書きなさい。

____ 1. One in every 27 people in Finland owns a summer cottage.

____ 2. When Finnish lakes are frozen in winter, you can walk on them.

____ 3. Santa Claus Village is located in Finland's far north.

● Grammar Section ●

関係代名詞

Grammar Points

関係代名詞は先行詞を修飾する関係節（形容詞節）を導きます。who（人）/ which（人以外）/ that（人・人以外）などが用いられます。目的格の関係代名詞は省略可能で、先行詞を含む関係代名詞 what は名詞節を導きます。

① I have **a daughter who** is a lawyer.

② This is **the letter** (**that** [**which**]) he sent me yesterday.

③ She is **the only girl** (**who** [**that**]) I like in my class.

④ **The house that** [**which**] stands over there is my father's.

⑤ I don't believe **what** he said last week.

Exercise 1 (　) 内に入る最も適切な語を選びなさい。

1. I know a student (who / which / what) speaks Finnish very well.
2. Where is the sweater (who / that / what) I bought in Sweden?
3. (Who / Which / What) I need most is your advice on overseas travel.

Exercise 2 (　) 内に適切な関係代名詞を入れなさい。

1. This is a typical sauna (　　　　　　　　) you often see in Finland.
2. The only teacher (　　　　　　　　) has studied in Europe is Mr. Brown.
3. Tell me (　　　　　　　　) the child said in her letter to Santa Claus.

● Writing Section ●

「外国の紹介」に関わる表現

Exercise 1 下の語群から適当な語を選んで、文を完成させなさい。

1. This is the most beautiful lake (　　　　　　　　　) I have ever seen.
2. The menu is in Finnish. Would you please translate (　　　　　　　　　) it says here?
3. Some people (　　　　　　　　　) live in Finland speak Swedish.

who	what	that

Exercise 2 (　) 内の語を並べかえて英文を完成させなさい。

1. フィンランド人は石製のサウナが大好きです。(that / saunas / are)
   Finns love ______________________________ made of stones.
2. 私は Kristina が私に作ってくれたカレリアパイを食べているところです。(for / made / Kristina)
   I'm eating a Karelian pie that ______________________________ me.
3. ラップランドの白夜は私のいちばんの楽しみです。(enjoy / I / what)
   The midnight sun in Lapland is ______________________________ most.

Exercise 3 日本文を英語に直しなさい。

日本には約 1 億 2000 万人が住んでいます。

____

● Speaking Section ●

「困惑・心配」の表現

79

Exercise 1 強く発音するところの○ を黒く塗りつぶしなさい。次に CD を聞いてリピートし、英文を覚えなさい。

1. A: Excuse me, sir, but **I'm afraid** you took the wrong umbrella.
   ○　○○　○○　○　○　○　○　○　○
   B: Oh, I'm sorry, ma'am. They look so similar.
   ○　○　○　○　○　○　○○
2. A: Oh, you look a little pale. **Are you OK?** Shall I call a doctor?
   ○　○　○　○○　○　○　○　○　○○○○○
   B: No, thank you. I'm sure I'll feel better soon.
   ○　○　○○　○○　○　○　○

Exercise 2 日本語を参考にして、英語で言ってみましょう。

1. A: すみません、傘をお間違えのようですが。
   B: これはどうもすみません。よく似ているものですから。
2. A: おや、少し気分が悪そうですね。大丈夫ですか。医者を呼びましょうか。
   B: いえ結構です。すぐに良くなると思います。

Exercise 3 Exercise 1 の会話をペアで練習しなさい。

Unit 14 Education Overseas

● Listening Section ●

80

Listening Points

弱形と強形 —強く発音される can はどちら？—

前置詞、助動詞などは、通常「弱形」と呼ばれる強勢を持たない発音で聞こえます。しかし、重要な意味を持つ場合は単語本来の発音「強形」で発音されることもあります。

① Can you really swim 2 kilometers? — Yes, I can.
[kən/kn]（弱形）　[kæn]（強形）

② The book is on the table, isn't it? — No, it isn't on the table; it's under it.
[ən]（弱形）　[ɑn]（強形）

Exercise 1 CD を聞いて、絵について正しく描写している英文を選びなさい。 81

1. (a) (b) (c)

2. (a) (b) (c)

Exercise 2 CD を聞いて、質問に対する最も適切な応答を選びなさい。 82

1. (a) In Tokyo. (b) At the age of six. (c) They haven't started yet.
2. (a) Yes, I signed up yesterday. (b) I'll think it over. (c) No, but thanks for inviting me.

Exercise 3 CD を聞いて、次の設問に答えなさい。 83

1. Does the woman speak English well?
   (a) No, not at all.
   (b) Yes, but only a little.
   (c) Yes, very well.
2. What does the woman think about English now?
   (a) It is necessary to learn it.
   (b) Grammar is easy.
   (c) She dislikes it.

● Reading Section ●

Foreign Language Education Overseas

Words & Phrases 次の語句の日本語訳を選びなさい。

1. across the globe (　)　2. especially (　)　3. primary school (　)
4. for example (　)　5. needless to say (　)　6. popular (　)
7. in addition (　)　8. geography (　)　9. adopt (　)　10. practice (　)

(a) 人気のある　(b) 言うまでもなく　(c) 小学校　(d) 加えて　(e) 特に
(f) 世界中の　(g) 採り入れる　(h) 例えば　(i) 実践　(j) 地理

84

Reading Passage

English is now spoken worldwide by millions of non-native speakers. It is taught as a "second" language in schools all across the globe. In most countries, but especially in EU countries, children start learning English when they are in primary school.

In Italy, for example, English classes start in the first year of primary school. In Germany, some children start learning their first foreign language when they are in the third grade and others in the first grade. Needless to say, the most popular foreign language is English.

Many people in Europe are "plurilingual," which means that **they speak more than one language fluently**. Schools usually teach two or more foreign languages. In addition, CLIL programs, in which students learn math, history, or geography in a foreign language, are widely adopted these days.

Bilingual education, where two languages are used in the classroom, is a common educational practice in some countries. For example, both French and English are used in Canadian schools, and English and Spanish are used in classrooms in some U.S. states.

(174 words)

others in the first grade 第１学年から始める子もいる　plurilingual 多言語話者の　CLIL 内容言語統合型学習（Content and Language Integrated Learning: 外国語を用いて教科内容を学習すること。）　bilingual education 二言語教育（主に、児童・生徒の母語と当該国・地域の主要言語の両方が使用される）。

Exercise 1 ( ) 内に最も適切な語を選んで、文を完成させなさい。

1. English is the (   ) popular foreign language taught in the EU.
   (a) most (b) least (c) second most
2. In CLIL programs, students learn a subject like (   ) using a foreign language.
   (a) English (b) history (c) Japanese
3. In some U.S. schools, (   ) is also used in classrooms besides English.
   (a) French (b) German (c) Spanish

Exercise 2 次の各文が本文の内容に合っていれば T(True)、合っていなければ F(False) と書きなさい。

____ 1. In Italy, children's first foreign language class starts from the third year of primary school.

____ 2. Many people in Europe speak two languages or more.

____ 3. Bilingual education is found only in Canada.

● Grammar Section ●

関係副詞

Grammar Points

関係副詞は先行詞を修飾する関係節（形容詞節）を導き、関係節の中で、副詞の役割を果たします。when（時）・where（場所）・why（理由）・how（方法）の4種類があります。先行詞が内容により明らかな場合は、先行詞を省略できます（例文③④⑤）。

① Tell me **the day when** he will be back from Europe.
② I don't remember **the building where** I met them last Sunday.
③ This is **(the place) where** I was born.
④ That's **(the reason) why** I stopped smoking.
⑤ Show me **how** you cooked this meal.

Exercise 1 ( ) 内に入る最も適切な語を選びなさい。

1. Mondays and Fridays are the days (when / where / why) we have English class.
2. Let's study in a room (when / where / how) we can use computers.
3. He is going to study abroad soon. That's (where / why / how) he must study English so hard right now.

Exercise 2 ( ) 内に適切な関係副詞を入れなさい。

1. The city (   ) they live is famous for bilingual education.
2. Tell me the reason (   ) you are studying French.
3. I always read texts aloud. That's (   ) I study English.

● Writing Section ●

「海外の教育」に関わる表現

Exercise 1 下の語群から適当な語を選んで、文を完成させなさい。

1. I like (   ) the French language sounds.
2. Do you know a (   ) where they have adopted CLIL programs?
3. I still remember the time (   ) I first visited Europe.

when	how	school

Exercise 2 ( ) 内の語を並べかえて英文を完成させなさい。

1. こういう理由でケンは 3 歳で英語を学び始めました。(Ken / why / started)
   That's ______________________________ learning English at the age of three.
2. 彼女は数学を英語で教えている学校に通っています。(where / school / they)
   She attends a ______________________________ teach math in English.
3. みんなが英語を話す日がもうすぐやってくるでしょう。(day / everyone / when)
   The ______________________________ speaks English will soon come.

Exercise 3 日本文を英語に直しなさい。

私の姉は 3 つの言語を流暢《りゅうちょう》に話します。

____

● Speaking Section ●

「別れ」の表現

85

Exercise 1 強く発音するところの○を黒く塗りつぶしなさい。次に CD を聞いてリピートし、英文を覚えなさい。

1. A: Well, **I think I should leave now. Have a nice evening!**
   ○ ○ ○ ○ ○ ○ ○ ○ ○ ○ ○
   B: Thank you for coming. **Take care.**
   ○ ○ ○ ○ ○ ○
2. A: It was fun today. **See you tomorrow.**
   ○ ○ ○ ○ ○ ○ ○
   B: Yeah, I've had a great time, too. **Talk to you later. Bye.**
   ○ ○ ○ ○ ○ ○ ○ ○ ○ ○ ○

Exercise 2 日本語を参考にして、英語で言ってみましょう。

1. A: そろそろ失礼いたします。では、さようなら。
   B: 来てくださって、ありがとうございました。お気を付けて。
2. A: 今日は楽しかったです。また明日会いましょう。
   B: そうですね、私も大変楽しい一時を過ごさせていただきました。ではまた。さようなら。

Exercise 3 Exercise 1 の会話をペアで練習しなさい。

Appendix

Grammar Points

Unit 1　名詞・代名詞

（練習問題は 11 ページ）

▶ 名詞には数えられる名詞（可算名詞）と数えられない名詞（不可算名詞：advice, homework, furniture など）があります。

可算名詞	単数形（a ~ / an ~） 複数形（~s / ~es）	I have a **class** today. He has three **classes** today.
不可算名詞	water, the water, some water a glass of ~ などを用いて数えます	I want some **water**, please. Give him a glass of **water**.

▶ 代名詞は名詞の代わりに用いられます。前に出た名詞の繰り返しを避けるために使われます。
I am taking a math class. **It** (=The math class) is very interesting.

Unit 2　5 文型

（練習問題は 15 ページ）

▶ 英語の文は動詞を中心に成り立ち、構成要素の組み合わせによって 5 つの文型に分けられます。

第 1 文型	主語＋動詞（修飾語句を伴うことが多い。）	**Vegetables grew** in my garden.
第 2 文型	主語＋動詞＋補語（補語は名詞もしくは形容詞）（［主語＝補語］の関係が成り立つ）	**Growing vegetables is** not **easy.**
第 3 文型	主語＋動詞＋目的語（名詞もしくは代名詞など）	**He ate** fresh **vegetables**.
第 4 文型	主語＋動詞＋間接目的語［主に人］＋直接目的語［主に物］	**He gave me** some **vegetables**.
第 5 文型	主語＋動詞＋目的語＋補語（目的語＝補語の関係が成り立つ）	**He found gardening interesting.**

Unit 3　現在・過去・未来

（練習問題は 19 ページ）

▶「動詞」が表す動作や状態がいつ起こったかという時間的概念は「動詞」の語形によって表します。

現在形	現在の事実	They **are** foreign tourists. A train **is** a popular vehicle.
	現在の習慣・反復的行為	I **go** to college by bus. / He often **travels** abroad.
	普遍的真理・ことわざ	Water **boils** at 100°C. / All roads **lead** to Rome.
	未来の代用	Please call me when you **arrive** there.
過去形	過去の動作・状態	We **traveled** to Britain last year. I **was** on the train at that time.
	過去の習慣・反復的行為	I **enjoyed** traveling to unfamiliar places. She seldom **traveled** by plane.

Unit 4　進行形

（練習問題は 23 ページ）

▶ 進行形「be 動詞 + ing」は限られた期間の間だけ進行する動作や状態を表します。

現在進行形	主語 + is/are + 現在分詞	I **am swimming** now.
過去進行形	主語 + was/were + 現在分詞	I **was swimming** when you called me.
未来進行形	主語 + will be + 現在分詞	The plane **will be landing** shortly.

Unit 5 完了形

(練習問題は 27 ページ)

▶ 完了形は「have/has/had + 過去分詞」は、時間軸上のある時点を基準として、その時点までの動作の完了、継続、経験、結果を表します。

現在完了	主語 + have/has + 過去分詞	I **have lived** here for 5 years.(継続)
過去完了	主語 + had + 過去分詞	I **had** never **fallen** in love before I met you.(経験)
未来完了	主語 + will have + 過去分詞	I **will have finished** the work by tomorrow.(完了)

Unit 6 助動詞

(練習問題は 31 ページ)

▶ 助動詞は動詞に未来、可能、推量などの意味を加える役割をします。

will	～だろう(未来)	It **will** snow around Christmas.
	～するつもりである(意志未来)	I'**ll** invite you for Thanksgiving.
can	～できる(可能)	We **can** have a BBQ in the park.
	(否定文で)～のはずがない(否定推量)	That **cannot** be a ghost.
may	～かもしれない(推量)	He **may** come to the party.
	～してよい(許可)	**May** I unwrap the presents?
must	～しなければならない(義務)	You **must** follow the rules.
	～にちがいない(推量)	That story **must** be true.
	(否定文で)～してはいけない(禁止)	You **must** not open the present.
should	～すべきだ(義務)	You **should** try it.

Unit 7　不定詞

（練習問題は 35 ページ）

▶ 不定詞は「to + 動詞の原形」で表され、文中の機能によって 3 つの用法があります。

名詞的用法	文の主語、目的語、補語になる	I want **to go** to America.
形容詞的用法	名詞 / 代名詞を後から修飾する	She needs something hot **to drink**.
副詞的用法	動詞・形容詞・副詞を修飾する	We went to the library **to study**.

＊ 原形不定詞とは「to のつかない不定詞」で、知覚動詞（see, hear, feel）や使役動詞（make, have, let）などと一緒に使用されます。

I saw her leave the room.（私は彼が部屋から出て行くのを見た）　.

Please let me know.（私にお知らせ下さい）

▶ 不定詞は「to + 動詞の原形」で表され、文中の機能によって 3 つの用法があります。

▶ 不定詞だけを目的語にとる動詞　want, learn, hope, expect, manage, pretend, promise など

Unit 8　動名詞

（練習問題は 39 ページ）

▶ 動名詞は「動詞 + ing」で表され、通常の名詞と同じく文の主語・目的語・補語になります。

＊ 動名詞は前置詞の目的語としても使われます。

▶ 動名詞だけを目的語にとる動詞　finish, enjoy, mind, avoid, give up, postpone, escape など

Unit 9　受動態

（練習問題は 43 ページ）

▶ 能動態の文を受動態の文にするには、目的語 (O) を主語 (S) にし、動詞 (V) を「be ＋ 過去分詞」の形に変えて作ります。

能動態の文型	能動態	受動態
S V O	Some people **eat** various kinds of fish.	Various kinds of fish **are eaten** by some people.
S V O O	My mother **made** me French fries.	French fries **were made** for me by my mother.
S V O C	Music **keeps** me healthy.	I **am kept** healthy by music.

▶ 助動詞＋ V 原形の受動態は、「助動詞 ＋ be（の変化形） ＋ 過去分詞」の形に変えます。

能動態	受動態
Many people **can eat** the special food.	The special food **can be eaten** by many people.
The chef **will send** me a menu.	A menu **will be sent** to me by the chef.

Unit 10　前置詞

（練習問題は 47 ページ）

▶ 前置詞は名詞・代名詞の前に置かれ、名詞や動詞を修飾する句を作ります。

at	時の一点（**at** 4 p.m.）／場所の一点（**at** the corner）
in	時間の中（**in** the evening）／空間の中（**in** the house）／手段（**in** Japanese）
on	曜日（**on** Sunday）／日付（**on** June 14）／接触（**on** the ceiling）
for	継続期間（**for** two weeks）／方向（**for** Tokyo）／理由（**for** this reason）
by	期限（**by** the deadline）／近接（**by** my side）／手段（**by** taxi）
until	継続の終了点（**until** [**till**] next week）

＊ because of や in spite of などのように 2 語以上で前置詞の役割を果たすものもあります。

Unit 11　接続詞

（練習問題は 51 ページ）

▶ 接続詞には文法上対等関係にある語・句・節をつなぐ等位接続詞と、主節と従属節をつなぐ従位接続詞があります。

等位接続詞	語 / 句 / 節 + 接続詞 + 語 / 句 / 節	I quit smoking, **and** I am healthy now.
従位接続詞	主節 + 接続詞 + 従属節	I quit smoking **because** the doctor told me to.

＊ 等位接続詞：and, or, but, so, for など

＊ 従位接続詞（名詞節を導く）：that, if, whether など（従属節は主語・目的語・前の名詞と同格などの働きをする）

＊ 従位接続詞（時の副詞節を導く）：when, as, while など（while は対比、as は比例・理由・譲歩の意味もあります）

＊ 従位接続詞（条件の副詞節を導く）：if, unless, once など

＊ 従位接続詞（譲歩の副詞節を導く）：though, although, whether など

＊ 従位接続詞（理由の副詞節を導く）：because, since など

▶ both A and B, either A or B, so 形容詞・副詞 that のように 2 語で成り立つ接続詞もあります。

Unit 12　比較

（練習問題は 55 ページ）

▶ 2 つを比べる場合比較級を、3 つ以上を比べる場合最上級を使います。

比較級	最上級
形容詞、副詞＋ er または more ＋形容詞、副詞	the + 形容詞、副詞 + est または the + most + 形容詞、副詞
音節の少ない語（big（1 音節）early（2 音節））～ er, the ～ est 音節の多い語（beautiful（3 音節））more ～ , the most ～	
My dog is bigger than yours.	He is the **tallest** in the soccer team.
The actress is more beautiful than her.	This is the **most difficult** problem in life.
This train runs faster than the bus.	She arrived home the **earliest** among family members.

Unit 13　関係代名詞

（練習問題は 59 ページ）

▶ 関係代名詞は接続詞と代名詞の機能をあわせ持ち、2 つの文を 1 つにまとめることができます。

▶ 関係代名詞は先行詞の種類や関係節内での文法的機能によっていくつかの種類があります。

先行詞の種類	主格	所有格	目的格
人	who	whose	who/(whom)
人以外	which	whose	which

＊ 主格と目的格の関係代名詞は that で代用できます（ただし、先行詞に最上級や only などの強調表現が含まれる場合は that が優先されます）。目的格の関係代名詞は省略されることが多く、特に口語ではこの傾向が顕著です。

▶ what は先行詞を含む関係代名詞で the thing(s) which, anything that などの意味で用いられ、文の主語・目的語・補語となる名詞節を導きます。

What (= The thing which) you need most is some rest.

I will do **what** (= anything that) I can do.

▶ 先行詞の意味を限定する用法を制限用法、先行詞についての追加的な説明をする用法を非制限用法と呼びます。

I have two sons who became doctors.（息子が他にもいる含意がある）

I have two sons, who became doctors.（息子は 2 人のみである）

Unit 14　関係副詞

（練習問題は 63 ページ）

▶ 関係副詞とは接続詞と副詞の機能を持つ語で、先行詞の表す内容により 4 種類あります。

先行詞	関係副詞	例文
時	when	I remember the day **when** you won the award.
場所	where	This is the school **where** I studied.
理由	why	Explain the reason **why** you passed the exam.
方法	how	Explain **how** you passed the exam.

＊ 関係副詞を使った文で先行詞が当然わかる場合、先行詞を省略できます。

I know (the place) where we got together. I know (the time) when we should get together.

＊ 方法を表す how の場合、先行詞 (the way) か関係副詞の両方を使うことはできません。

Explain the way you passed the exam. = Explain how you passed the exam.

大学英語教育学会（JACET）
リスニング研究会
代表　　神野　雅代
執筆者　岩井　麻紀
　　　　梶浦　眞由美
　　　　神野　雅代
　　　　柴田　かよ子
　　　　高橋　寿夫
　　　　林　姿穂
　　　　松村　優子
　　　　米崎　啓和

Power-Up College English <Intro>　[NSS-23]
パワーアップ・イングリッシュ〈入門編〉

第 1 刷　2021 年 4 月 1 日
第 2 刷　2023 年 9 月 15 日

著　者　JACET リスニング研究会
発行者　南雲　一範　Kazunori Nagumo
発行所　株式会社　南雲堂
〒 162-0801　東京都新宿区山吹町 361
NAN'UN-DO CO.,Ltd.
361 Yamabuki-cho, Shinjuku-ku, Tokyo 162-0801, Japan
振替口座：00160-0-46863
TEL：03-3268-2311(営業部：学校関係)
TEL：03-3268-2384(営業部：書店関係)
TEL：03-3268-2387(編集部)
FAX：03-3269-2486
編集者　加藤　敦
イラスト　パント　大吉
装　丁　N スタジオ
組　版　堀田　華
検　印　省略
コード　ISBN 978-4-523-18523-9　C0082

Printed in Japan

E-mail　nanundo@post.email.ne.jp
URL　https://www.nanun-do.co.jp